ISADORA SPEAKS

ISADORA SPEAKS

ISADORA DUNCAN

ᴐꜩᴐ

Edited and introduced by
Franklin Rosemont

City Lights Books
San Francisco

Cover photograph: The Dover Street Studios, London. Courtesy of The Bancroft Library, University of California, Berkeley

Frontispiece: Courtesy, *The Dance,* June, 1926

Second printing: February 1983

Library of Congress Cataloging in Publication Data

Duncan, Isadora, 1878-1927.
  Isadora speaks.

  Contents: Introduction/by Franklin
Rosemont—Reminiscences of childhood—
Dance and the new woman—[etc.]
    1. Duncan, Isadora, 1878-1927—Addresses,
essays, lectures. 2. Dancers—United States—
Biography—Addresses, essays, lectures.
I. Rosemont, Franklin. II. Title.
GV1785.D8A25   1981   793.3'2'0924 [B] 81-21692
ISBN 0-87286-134-1   AACR2
ISBN 0-87286-133-3 (pbk.)

Designed by Nancy Joyce Peters

CITY LIGHTS BOOKS are edited by Lawrence Ferlinghetti and Nancy J. Peters, and published at the City Lights Bookstore, 261 Columbus Avenue, San Francisco, California 94133

This Book is Dedicated to
SYBIL SHEARER
Brave Exemplar of Marvelous Freedom

&

to the Memory of
HELENE VANEL
Danseuse surréaliste

CONTENTS

INTRODUCTION: ISADORA FOREVER!

Dancer, adventurer, revolutionist, ardent defender of the poetic spirit, Isadora Duncan (1877-1927) has been one of the most enduring influences on twentieth century culture. Ironically, the very magnitude of her achievements as an artist, as well as the sheer excitement and tragedy of her life, have tended to dim our awareness of the originality, depth and boldness of her thought. But Isadora always was a thinker as well as a doer, gifted with a lively poetic imagination, critical lucidity, a radical defiance of "things as they are," and the ability to express her ideas with verve and humor.

This volume brings together, for the first time, dozens of her essays, speeches, interviews, letters-to-the-editor and statements to the press that until now have remained inaccessible in old newpapers, obscure periodicals and out-of-print books. This material adds to our understanding of Isadora as dancer and theorist of dance; as critic of modern society, culture, education; and as champion of the struggles for women's rights, social revolution and the realization of poetry in everyday life.

Born in San Francisco, Isadora spent her childhood in the Bay Area in the years that a wide-ranging aggregate of poets, artists and inspired "characters" were turning the former gold-rush settlement into one of the most vital creative centers in the world. In the raucous, free-wheeling ethos that brought forth *The Call of the Wild* and *The Devil's Dictionary*, Isadora provoked the "awakening," as she put it, of "an art that has slept for two thousand years." Virtually alone, she restored *dance* to a high place among the arts.

Breaking with all conventions, Isadora traced the art of dance back to its roots as a *sacred* art—universally symbolic of the act of creation. With characteristic lack of equivocation, she proclaimed herself "an enemy of ballet"—an enemy, indeed, of all the insipid dance of her time. She scorned the restrictive garb and other artifices of the stage-dancer, and developed free and natural movements. In her diaphanous tunic and bare feet, she restored to the human body its vital actuality as an expressive instrument. Her celebrated "simplicity" was oceanic in its depth. Returning to ancient modes of apprehension relating bodily movements to cosmogony and magic, Isadora invented what later came to be known as *modern dance*.

Her success in this domain, of course, needs no emphasis. Within a few years she became the inspiration of millions of people, including the leading poets and artists of her time. She danced in dozens of countries before audiences rarely if ever exceeded. Indeed, she is the only dancer who can truly be called, in Hegel's sense, a *world-historical figure*.

Interestingly, Hegel in his *Aesthetics* classified dance among the "imperfect arts," along with gardening.[1] But the most encyclopedic man of an encyclopedic age nonetheless conceded at least the *possibility* of dance as a major vehicle of human expression:

> If some spiritual expression is to glint through this mere dexterity, which nowadays has wandered into an extreme of senselessness and intellectual poverty, what is required is not only a complete conquest of all the technical difficulties but measured movement in harmony with our emotions, and a freedom and grace that are extremely rare.[2]

Does this not read like a veritable prophecy of our young Californian? Significantly, this striking passage occurs in Hegel's discussion of *poetry*, the "universal art" which embraces the totality of the human spirit and unifies all forms of artistic expression. Among the arts, poetry was the first to comprehend the modern spirit; dance was the last. Throughout the modern period dance has been, as Doris Humphrey observed, "ten to fifty years behind the other arts."[3] The reasons for this retardation are not difficult to discern. The poetic instrument is the *word*, the most portable of all substances, and the least affected by repression. In dance, however, the instrument is precisely the *body*, on which repression is most heavily concentrated.

It is no accident, in any case, that Isadora was inspired not by dancers—much less by "dance masters"—but, on the contrary, by *poets*! Blake, Whitman, Rousseau, Nietzsche, Keats, Shelley, Byron, Poe, the Pre-Raphaelites, the great French Romantics and Symbolists: These were key sources of the new dance. Isadora situated herself in that grand poetic tradition which—from Shakespeare and the great Elizabethans all the way to the surrealists—is distinguished above all by its insistence on the primacy of the *unfettered imagination*.

She was influenced, too, by painters, sculptors and musicians. A close student of everything alive in ancient and "classical" art, she became an inspiration to innovative currents as varied as the New York "Ashcan School," the Yiddish "Die Yunge," Italian Futurism, Russian Imaginism and Parisian Dadaism. She who revolutionized the art of dance began by assimilating the revolutions in other forms of expression. The first to apply poetic imperatives to dance, she in turn became a major influence on poetry and the other arts.

☽

Isadora had the highest hopes for dance—as an art, as a new educational force, and even as a means of social transformation. But she did not regard herself, and did not wish to be regarded by others, as "merely a dancer." Her approach never was narrowly esthetic; her aspirations went far beyond the stage. *Revolt* was the hallmark of all that she did. "I am not a dancer," she insisted. "What I am interested in doing is finding and expressing a new form of life."

Exceptionally rebellious even as a child, Isadora grew more radical each passing year. Her unconventional dance inevitably brought her into conflict with the forces of puritanism and other manifestations of cultural/political sclerosis. Like most authentic poets, she repeatedly found herself in trouble with the police, and slandered in the bourgeois press. The insults hurled at her by Bible-thumping evangelists, tinhorn politicians, the American Legion and the Ku Klux Klan—not to mention aristocratic patrons of ballet—doubtless helped her develop a critique of capitalist/christian hypocrisy, and led her to identify herself with currents seeking radical social change. Her motto, she affirmed, was *"sans limites,"* and she set out to combat the limits imposed by bourgeois law'n'order. With the same freedom and grace that characterized her dance, she took up the whole gamut of radical and revolutionary causes.

Isadora's social views covered a wide field, indeed—her "program" included at one time or another everything from dress reform to vegetarianism to birth control. But her radicalism was by no means flighty or frivolous, as some critics have pretended. On the contrary, she demonstrated over a long period a serious, consistent and practical dedication to the struggles she upheld as particularly her own: the women's movement; opposition to organized religion; a new educational system; and the abolition of wage-slavery.

Throughout her life she was a vigorous exemplar of woman's emancipation, and her writings are important documents of that struggle. To our knowledge, she never called herself a feminist, or belonged to any feminist group, but it is not surprising that she came into contact with Antoinette Konikow, Sylvia Pankhurst, Alexandra Kollontai and Klara Zetkin, whose program for women's liberation included socialist revolution. Isadora always maintained that her dance was, more than anything else, "symbolic of the freedom of woman." She looked ahead bravely to the coming "new woman . . . more glorious than any woman that has yet been . . . the highest intelligence in the freest body!"

Brought up in a free-thinking family, Isadora remained a sharp critic of organized religion. This did not prevent her from invoking now and then the central figures in various ancient religious myths. Moreover, like Shelley, Rimbaud, Breton and other poets noted for their vehement atheism, she was deeply interested in "occult" theories, heretical doctrines and psychical research. Like the poets, she trespassed on religious ground whenever it pleased her to do so, and for purely poetic purposes. Always she could have declared, with Luis Buñuel, "I'm still an atheist, thank God!"

Isadora's views on education were developed in considerable detail; undoubtedly they comprise her most original work as a social theorist. Taking as her point of departure her own school experiences as a child, which she recalled were "as humiliating as a penitentiary," reflecting "a brutal incomprehension of childhood," she elaborated a profound critique of modern educational institutions which even today, alas! has lost none of its timeliness. Her own School was designed to be completely different from, and opposed to, all other schools. She did not regard it as a "school of dance," in the usual sense, but rather as a kind of organizing center for what she called a "general reform of the world." In her educational ideas, Isadora rejoins the great utopians, especially Charles Fourier, genial theorist of *passional attraction.*

Political radicals of all kinds—anarchists, socialists, single-taxers—long constituted a majority of her friends, but Isadora's own radicalism did not assume a clear political orientation until relatively late in her life. She was profoundly affected by what she saw of the aftermath of "Bloody Sunday" during the Russian

Revolution of 1905, and it was the overthrow of Czarism twelve years later that led her to begin thinking of herself as a communist. "On the night of the Russian Revolution," she wrote in *My Life*, "I danced with a terrible fierce joy." During the last years of her life, her allegiance to the cause of the Third International was unwavering.

To make Isadora appear more "respectable," some commentators have scoffed at, or even entirely ignored, her avowed support for the workers' movement. Fortunately, however, it is impossible to misread her own crystal-clear pronouncements on the subject. In the great contest between Capital and Labor, Isadora left not the smallest doubt as to which side she was on. "In my red tunic," she wrote, "I have always danced the Revolution."

It is true that she was little inclined to the narrower varieties of ideological disputation, and it seems unlikely that she made much of an effort to master the finer points of Marxist theory. Her adherence to the revolutionary cause may have been largely romantic and even utopian—but in the best sense of those terms. Disdaining the old forms of address, "Miss" and "Mademoiselle," she insisted on being called Comrade. Her zeal for Bolshevik Russia, for Lenin, for the International, was beyond question. Later, as the workers' councils succumbed to blows from the vast privileged bureaucracy consolidated by Stalin (who, incidentally, admired the decadent ballet), she grew more critical. But her solidarity with the basic aims and achievements of the Revolution never diminished; indeed, it grew continually stronger.

The fact that she never joined any revolutionary organization does not mean that her support for revolution was merely verbal. On the contrary, Isadora was always very much an activist. In the early 1900s, long before Dadaism systematized such provocations, she harangued the youth of Berlin to tear down the ugly militaristic statues that disfigured that city's parks. She who could write so lyrically of the workers' May Day was a ready participant in street demonstrations. She agitated for Russian famine-relief, for the independence of Ireland, for the release of class war prisoners. Near the end of her life her Paris apartment served as meetingplace for the committee to defend Sacco and Vanzetti, and she herself took an active part in the tumultuous protests against the judicial murder of these two anarchist workers.

Isadora's greatest services to the revolution, of course, lay elsewhere—in her dance, her teaching, her *example*. These were her own unique contributions to the overthrow of the old society and the building of the new. That she herself tended to view them in this light is made plain in many of her utterances. But how few critics have been willing to admit that this great dancer intended her life's work to be, not a source of amusement for the rich, but a lever of human emancipation!

Not one of Isadora's biographers has mentioned the efforts of Juliette Poyntz, of the International Ladies' Garment Workers Union in New York, in 1915, to establish a school for working-class children under Isadora's direction. The project regrettably did not materialize; her School was always plagued with misfortune. Even later when, with the aid of the Soviet government, she opened a School in Moscow, it fell far short of her hopes. She dreamed of a big School, with a thousand children in spacious surroundings. But like Fourier's Phalanstery, Isadora's School remained more dream than reality. It persists nonetheless, like the dream of Fourier, on a near-mythic plane, as a grand appeal for a life made marvelous. For Isadora's vision did not stop at a School; the School, for her, was only a beginning. To Walt Whitman's "I hear America singing," she added "I see America dancing." Internationalist that she was, she could truly have said that she saw the *whole world* dancing.

In her dance, in her teaching, in her life, Isadora communicated a wildly generous, all-embracing revolutionary spirit, a passionate enthusiasm for a new and exalted life of creativity and freedom. Some idea of the *universality* implicit in her revolutionary élan—her ability to transcend the temporal, sectarian, strategic and tactical differences that divide those whose common aim is to transform the world—may be gauged from the enthusiasm that she and her work evoked in partisans whose views were otherwise strongly opposed. We know that Lenin, for instance, "liked Isadora Duncan very much," and that he was "deeply interested" in her work. "The more attention we pay to what she is doing," he said, "the better the results will be."[4] She was also a good friend of the anarchist Alexander Berkman. An outspoken critic of Bolshevism, Berkman was a warm admirer of Isadora's, and called her "a great and noble character."[5] But perhaps it was the socialist Floyd Dell, writing in the *The Masses* in 1916, who best expressed the ardor Isadora inspired for a whole generation of radicals:

> A strange and dark century, the nineteenth! . . . It does not console me to remember that through that darkness there flamed such meteors as Nietzsche and Whitman, Darwin and Marx, prophetic of the splendors of millennium. When I think that if I had lived and died in the darkness of that century I should never have seen with these eyes the beauty and terror of the human body, I am glad of the daylight of my own time. It is not enough to throw God from his pedestal, and dream of superman and the co-operative commonwealth: One must have *seen* Isadora Duncan to die happy.[6]

℧

Isadora did not think of herself as a writer; in *My Life* she bemoaned the fact that she lacked "the pen of a Cervantes or even of a Casanova." In truth, she wrote and spoke with clarity, and a sparkle all her own. *My Life* is probably the most widely read autobiography in the English language, after Benjamin Franklin's. Surely no *dancer* has had so much to say, and has said it so well, on such a wide range of subjects.

Too many biographies of Isadora have reduced her to carica-
ture, or legend, or a mere fragment of her true self. Here she is *in
her own words:* anti-puritanical, eros-affirming, libertarian, radical
in everything, an authentic *free spirit,* one of the boldest con-
temners of miserabilism in all its forms—an inspiration for all
who dream of a better world, all who strive to make that dream a
reality.

Franklin Rosemont

Chicago
November 1981

NOTES

1   G.W.F. Hegel: *Aesthetics—Lectures on Fine Art.* Translated by T.M.Knox. (Lon-
    don, Oxford University Press, 1975), Volume II, p. 627.

2   *Ibid.,* p. 1192.

3   Doris Humphrey: *The Art of Making Dances.* (N.Y., Grove Press; 1959), p. 174.

4   Quoted in Ilya Ilyich Schneider: *Isadora Duncan—The Russian Years.* (N.Y.,
    Harcourt, 1968), p. 44.

5   Richard and Anna Maria Drinnon, eds.:   *Nowhere at Home—Letters from Exile of
    Emma Goldman and Alexander Berkman.* (N.Y., Schocken, 1975), pp. 125-6.

6   Floyd Dell: "Who Said That Beauty Passes Like a Dream?" Reprinted in his
    Looking at Life. (N.Y., Knopf, 1924), p. 49.

ACKNOWLEDGMENTS

Thanks to Russell Hartley of the Archives for the Performing Arts; the Dance Collection of the New York Public Library at Lincoln Center; the Chicago Historical Society; Special Collections, Northwestern University Library, in Evanston; the Bancroft Library, University of California in Berkeley; and John Rammel of the Milwaukee *Journal* for help in locating some of the material reprinted here; to Leah Dillon Grant for permission to reproduce her watercolors by Abraham Walkowitz; to Lawrence Ferlinghetti, Anne Janowitz, and Nancy Joyce Peters for their encouragement and aid throughout the preparation of this book; and to my wife Penelope who, a decade or more ago, urged me to read Isadora's autobiography, thereby sparking an interest that has steadily grown.

F.R.

REMINISCENCES
OF
CHILDHOOD

Photograph by Eichenbacher, Oakland, 1880

"I am called Isadora. That means
Child of Isis—or Gift of Isis."

"It is certainly to this wildly untrammeled life of my child-hood," Isadora wrote in *My Life,* "that I owe the inspiration of the dance I created, which was but the expression of freedom. I was never subjected to the continual *don'ts* which it seems to me make children's lives a misery."

Of Scotch and Irish ancestry, Isadora was born in San Francisco on 26 May 1877. She remained in the Bay Area till 1896, later making her home in Chicago, New York, England, France, Greece, Germany and Soviet Russia. Her parents were separated when she was still a young child, but the rest of the family was remarkably close-knit. Her two brothers, Augustin and Raymond, and her sister Elizabeth also pursued careers in the theater arts.

In the first two chapters of her autobiography she recounted her early years in detail, and touched on the subject frequently in her other writings and speeches. Two of the reminiscences here—"I Was Born in America" and "Continually Surrounded by Flames"—date from her Soviet Russian sojourn in the 1920s. The first is from a transcript of a speech delivered at a Moscow theater; the second is part of a draft of an autobiography. "Childhood in San Francisco" is part of an interview published shortly after Isadora's arrival in Greece in 1903.

Isadora on tour. Photograph by Kervel, Fresno, 1889

I WAS BORN IN AMERICA

I was born in America in the city of San Francisco on the day when a revolution broke out there. The revolution, of course, was a "golden" one; it was the "golden" day when all the banks in San Francisco went bankrupt. Furious crowds raged in the streets. From one moment to the next, on the day of that catastrophe, my mother expected my birth. She told me later that she was sure that the child she expected would be something extraordinary in life. It so happens that my father was involved in this bankers' catastrophe. Our house was surrounded by a menacing crowd, and my mother was sure that all this worry, excitement and fear would have some effect on the child she was expecting. That is why she believed that I was going to be something extraordinary.

After these tempestuous days, my mother was abandoned to fate with four small children on her hands. Although she was an educated woman, she was barely able to earn a bit of bread for herself and her children by giving music lessons. Her earnings were small and not enough to feed us. Whenever I remember my childhood, I see before me an empty house. With my mother at her lessons, we children sat by ourselves, generally hungry, and in winters generally cold.

But even though our mother couldn't give us enough physical food, she did give us enough spiritual food. When she played Schubert and Beethoven for us, or read to us from Shakespeare and Shelley and Browning, we forgot our hunger and cold.

As a child I had no toys or childish fun. I often ran away alone into the woods or to the beach by the sea, and there I danced. I felt even then that my shoes and my clothes only hindered me. My heavy shoes were like chains; my clothes were my prison. So I took everything off. And without any eyes watching me, entirely alone, I danced, naked by the sea. And it seemed to me as if the sea and all the trees were dancing with me.

Since my mother was very poor, and we frequently lacked money even for necessities, our neighbors—knowing of my dancing ability—urged my mother to let me dance before the public, so that I could earn money. And so, out of necessity, I—a four-year-old child—was forced to dance before the public. That is why I don't like children to dance before the public for money, because I myself have experienced what it means to dance for a piece of bread.

[1924]

CHILDHOOD IN SAN FRANCISCO

I was brought up in San Francisco, where my father's house* was plentifully supplied with reproductions of classic art in sculpture and engraving. In this artistic atmosphere I breathed the first years of my childhood. There I became inspired with high artistic ideals, and while a little girl my inborn taste for dancing was developed.

While playing in the garden of my father's house, I tried by instinct to impart to my childish dance what I saw exhibited in the models of art. Thus deeply imbued with the perfect beauty of the copies of great masterpieces, enhanced by the simplicity of the dress, from my early childhood I have considered the freedom of my body essential to the rhythm of movement. For this reason later on, with the development of my inborn disposition, a conscious study of the rhythm was at the same time promoted. Dressed in the beautiful ancient dresses, I went on in the mode of dancing which I felt ambitious to render equal in beauty to the Greek dances of the days of old.

[Greece, 1903]

---

* House in which Isadora was born, at the corner of Geary and Taylor streets. By the time she was four, her mother had left Joseph C. Duncan and moved with the children to Oakland.

CONTINUALLY SURROUNDED BY FLAMES

Like the family of the Atreids* there are strains of blood whose life seems continuously enveloped in tragedy.

The gods sell their gifts dearly. For every joy there is a corresponding agony. For what they give of Fame, Wealth, Love, they extract Blood and Tears and grinding Sorrow. I am continually surrounded by flames.

My first recollection—a clear sensual remembrance of being thrown from a burning window to the arms of a policeman, and I hear the shrieks of my mother:"My boys, my boys! Let me go back for them!" Often at night I hear the voice of my father shouting: "Courage! They will come to save us." He met his death clinging to the seat of an overturned rowboat in the wild waves off the rocks of Falmouth. Always fire and water and sudden fearful death.

Of my childhood entire memories stand out with extraordinary vividness; the rest is enclosed in darkness.

My mother raised four children by the precarious profession of music teaching. Her continually bothered and anxious face was so familar to us; we lived in a perpetual state of terror lest we hear the rat-ta-tat of disagreeable landlords on the door, asking for the rent, and in a continual changing of address from one lodging or small cottage to another.

I remember all through my childhood a distinct feeling of the general unpleasantness of life as being a normal condition. And a continual going to school with leaking shoes and unsatisfied stomach made learning impossible.

---

*   The legendary Greek House of Atreus was plagued by incest, murder, cannibalism, and intrigue.

I remember once, when I was about eight years old, the teacher asked each child for a story of their short lives. The other children's consisted of accounts of gardens, of toys, of pet dogs, etc. Mine ran somewhat as follows:

First we lived at 23rd Street in East Oakland. The man kept asking for the rent until we moved to a small house on 17th Street. But again we were not allowed to remain. In three months we moved to two small rooms on Sunpath Avenue. As Mama could not take the furniture, we had only one large bed for all. But again the unkind landlord became disagreeable, and we moved to . . . etc., etc. This continued through fifteen moves in two years.

The teacher thought I was playing a bad joke on her and summoned my mother to appear before the board of directors. When my mother read the "life" she burst into tears and said that I had written only the truth. I remember her eyes were red for days afterward, and I could not understand. The state in which we lived, continually hunted, had seemed to me the normal thing. I think that is why I have worked in the interest of government feeding and education and general welfare of children.

My mother not only taught music but knitted caps, jackets, etc. for the big store. I remember often waking at dawn and seeing my mother still knitting. What a life for her! The only bright spots were when she had a piano and would play for hours—Beethoven, Schubert, Mozart, Schumann; or she would read aloud to us from Shelley, Burns, Keats, many poems which she taught us to recite by heart. She taught us children to listen curled up on the rug at her feet.

At that time my mother was still young and beautiful but, cursed with the narrow bourgeois principles, she did not know how to use either her youth or beauty or indomitable intelligence or strength. She was in the prisonhouse of the days before the Emancipation of Women. Sentimental and virtuous, she could only suffer and weep. And young as we were, we too suffered, each in our way, and our pillows were often wet with the tears of children who go to bed hungry.

This is the Christian education which does not know how to teach children Nietzsche's superb phrase: "Be hard!" Only from an early age some spirit kept whispering to me to "be hard."

I remember coming in one day and finding mother crying on the bed and sobbing her heart out. About her were lying all the knitted things of a week's work, which she had not been able to sell at the stores. A sudden revolt possessed me. I decided I would sell these things for mother and at a good price. I put on one of the little red knitted capes and caps, and with the rest in a basket I set forth. From house to house I peddled my wares. Some people were kind, others rude. On the whole I had success, but it was the first awakening in my childish breast of the monstrous injustice of the world. And that little red knitted cap that my mother had made was the cap of a baby Bolshevik.

[1924]

NEW DANCE
NEW EDUCATION
NEW WOMAN

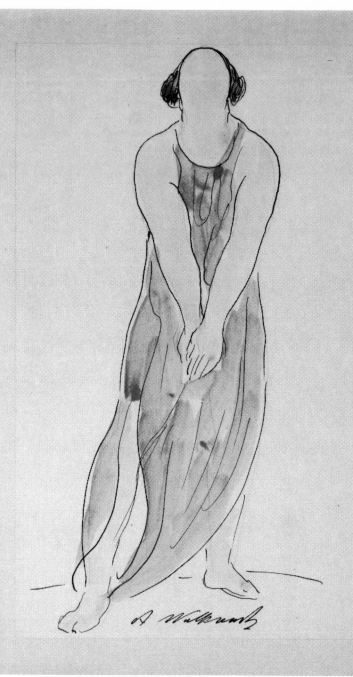

Watercolor by Abraham Walkowitz

"Dance waves sound waves light waves —all the same."

Isadora's views on woman's emancipation and the education of children are inseparable from her theory and practice of dance. In *The Art of the Dance* she wrote: "For me the dance is not only the art that gives expression to the human soul through movement, but also the foundation of a complete conception of life, more free, more harmonious, more natural." Once she summed it up aphoristically: "To dance is to live. What I want is a *school of life.*"

Like most high-spirited young people, Isadora hated school as a child. "When I could escape from the prison of school," she wrote in *My Life,* "I was free ... My real education came during the evenings when my mother played to us Beethoven, Schumann, Schubert, Mozart, Chopin, or read aloud to us from Shakespeare, Shelley, Keats or Burns. These hours were to us enchanted." On the basis of such early impressions she developed her critique of modern education, and her unconventional notion of what a school should be.

She envisioned her own School as the starting-point of nothing less than a global *crusade.* By means of her dance she would inspire a number of adepts who would, in their turn, inspire others; as this effort gained ground, it would help to radically change the world. She conceived this plan early in life, and held to it. Shortly before her death she predicted that "the day is coming when a grand international school of children ... will open the doors of the future to a new humanity."

Women were to play the initiating and leading role in this crusade. Isadora at age twelve, as she wrote in *My Life,* had resolved that she "would live to fight against marriage and for the emancipation of women," and throughout her life she defended an approach to feminism uniquely her own. "The chief thing," she argued, is that woman "must *live* this beauty, and her body must become the living exponent of it."

All material in this section was published during her lifetime.

Watercolor by Abraham Walkowitz

I HAVE A WILL OF MY OWN:
ADDRESS TO THE BERLIN PRESS CLUB

People sometimes reproach me with having neither genius nor talent, nor deep feeling, but I have a will of my own, and my will is to free the art of dancing from the unnatural contortions which are the product of the modern ballet, and to lead it back to natural movements.

How beautiful these movements are that we see in animals, plants, waves and winds. All things in nature have forms of motion corresponding to their innermost being. Primitive man still has such movements and, starting from that point, we must try to create beautiful movements significant of cultured man—a movement which, without spurning the laws of gravitation, sets itself in harmony with the motion of the universe.

The Greek dances were spontaneous and natural. We must seek to revive them. Not mere national dances, but _human_ dances.

Just as the nude is the highest in all art must it be the highest in the dance, for dancing is the ritual of the religion of physical beauty. The dancer of the future will have to suit the dance to the symmetry of the body. She must have a perfect body, which will again be recognized as beautiful, pure and holy. And in this body a free, great spirit must find harmonious utterance in the excitement of the dance. Only in this way can dancing be raised to its place among the fine arts.

[1903]

THE SECRET BEAUTY OF HER MOVEMENT:
LETTER TO THE *BERLIN MORGEN POST*

While reading your esteemed paper I was embarrassed to find that you had asked so many admirable masters of the dance to expend such profound thought on so insignificant a subject as my humble self. I feel that much literature has been wasted on so unworthy a theme. And I suggest that instead of asking them "Can Miss Duncan Dance?" you should have called their attention to a far more celebrated dancer—one who has been dancing in Berlin for years, long before Miss Duncan appeared: a natural dancer whose style (which Miss Duncan tries to follow) is also in direct opposition to today's school of ballet.

The dancer to whom I refer is the statue of the dancing Maenad in the Berlin Museum. Now will you kindly write again to the admirable masters and mistresses of the ballet and ask them, "Can the dancing Maenad dance?"

For the dancer of whom I speak has never tried to walk on the end of her toes. Neither has she spent time practicing leaps in the air to see how many times she could clap her heels together before coming down again. She wears neither corset nor tights, and her bare feet rest freely in her sandals.

I believe a prize has been offered to the sculptor who could replace the statue's broken arms in their original position. I suggest that it might be even more useful, for art today, to offer a prize to whoever could reproduce in life the heavenly poise of her body and the secret beauty of her movement. I suggest that your excellent paper might offer such a prize, and that the excellent ballet masters and mistresses could compete for it.

Perhaps, after years of trying, they will have learned something of human anatomy, something of the beauty, the purity, the intelligence of the movements of the human body. Breathlessly awaiting their learned reply, I remain

Sincerely yours,

Isadora Duncan

[1903]

Drawing of Isadora by Gordon Craig, 1905

MY IDEA OF DANCING

My idea of dancing is to leave my body free to the sunshine, to feel my sandaled feet on the earth, to be near and to love the olive trees of Grèece. These are my present ideas of dancing. Two thousand years ago a people lived here who had perfect sympathy and comprehension of the beautiful in Nature, and this knowledge and sympathy were perfectly expressed in their own forms and movement.

Of all the thousands of figures of Greek sculpture, bas-reliefs and vases, there is not one but is in exquisite bodily proportion and harmony of movement.

This could not be possible unless the artists of that time were accustomed to see always about them beautiful moving human forms. I came to Greece to study these forms of ancient art, but above all I came to live in the land which produced these wonders, and when I say "to live" I mean to dance.

Coming at last to this adored place, I find that the glory and the greatness are more even than my dreams. I am still dazzled. My dance at present is to lift my hands to the sky, to feel the glorious sunshine and to thank the gods that I am here.

What I have danced before was only a prayer to this arriving. What shall I dance in the future? It is not good to have too many theories as to that.

[Statement on arrival in Greece, 1903]

THE PURPOSE OF MY SCHOOL

During the last ten years of my work I have constantly had the clear intention of founding a school which would restore the dance to its former high level of art. From various signs I have noticed that this art is in the throes of a new awakening. There is a real longing in the world for rhythmic movements; in the young generation, especially among students, there is a very noticeable desire for physical expression through movement. Visible proof that I have not been mistaken in my assumption is the recognition which the general public has given to my own endeavors in this respect. Convinced that it only needed someone with a firm will to make a start in that direction and inspire others to help this great aim, which might develop into something really great in the future, I opened the new School of Dance in 1904.

To rediscover in its ideal form the beautiful rhythmic movements of the human body, in harmony with the highest beauty of physical form, and to resuscitate an art that has lain dormant for two thousand years—that is the serious purpose of my school.

[1907-08]

MUSIC AND DANCE

Music touches the heart, makes it vibrate with emotion. The dance is only at its beginning, in its infancy. Music is like a great strong goddess which leads the dance by the hand like a little child. Its rhythm, its soul, its harmony is life itself.

Plato in his *Republic* recognized that music is life and beauty. The study of music was one of the laws of the Republic, and it is essential to the balance and health of every man. If men now understood this thoroughly, we should have more of the right kind of music, more of the music we have had this evening. But we should not have so much of the other kind—the ragtime, the trivial foolish jingles which are heard so much in America.

Such music is disease and death, whereas that of Beethoven and Chopin and Schumann is life itself.

[Excerpts from a speech,
quoted in *Current Literature*,
New York, November 1908]

WHAT IS THERE LEFT?
SPEECH AT THE CENTURY OPERA HOUSE, NEW YORK

What is there left in America [for creative people] but the ships to take them to lands where their efforts are appreciated?

There are people here tonight that have paid as much as $100,000 for a painting by some Old Master of Europe. The cost of one of those paintings would support my school for a long time. I suppose that twenty-five years after I am dead they will come along and build an immense theater, just about as ugly as this one, and try to start the work that I am doing now. They will build the theater, but when they try to imitate me they will not know how to begin. They may get the same beautiful pictures, the same graceful movement of the limbs, the arms and the head, but the feeling will not be there.

These beautiful children you have seen tonight are doing things that have not been done for 2000 years. And remember, they are at what they call the awkward age, fifteen and sixteen. They are at the age when most people would dress them in corsets, high-heeled shoes, and send them out to tango. If they made the same movements tonight that are made in the average modern dance, you would all run out of the building.

My work is appreciated by those people in the gallery because only the poor people in this country are intelligent. Do you suppose someone is going to help me stay here? I want to build up my school in America. I want fifty boys and fifty girls to train and to teach them the love of things beautiful.

Isn't there someone in America to help me do this? I could build up a school for about one quarter of what this hideous theater cost. Only the rich people here can make it possible for me. But the rich people of America are so criminally unintelligent that it seems there is nothing left for me but to take the ship and emigrate.

[April 1915]

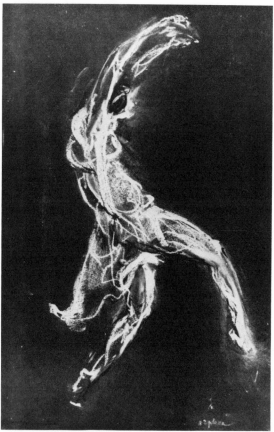

"Fury," a study by Jules Grandjouan
(Courtesy, The Bancroft Library, University of California, Berkeley)

THE DANCE AND ITS INSPIRATION:
Written in the Form of an Old Greek Dialogue

"We should learn that the body of woman has through all ⚡
the ages itself been the symbol of highest beauty." A
silence fell upon us. I was looking toward some light clouds
which had gathered in the east, and then it seemed to me in
their midst I saw a young goatherd sitting surrounded by
his goats and sheep of fleecy whiteness—and before him,
rose-tipped of the sun, stood the Goddess of Cyprus, and
she smiled as she reached her hand for the prize which she
knew was hers. That exquisitely poised head, those
shoulders gently sloping, those breasts firm and round, the
ample waist with its free lines, curving to the hips, those
limbs and knees and feet all one perfect whole, one instant
and the vision was radiant in its loveliness and then
vanished.

"To learn," I repeated, "that through all the ages woman's body has been the symbol of highest beauty."

"Will you explain to me what you mean?" you asked.

"Why," I replied, "is it not true that the first conception of
beauty arose from the consciousness of proportion, line,
the symmetry of the human form, for surely without this
consciousness we could have had no understanding of the
beauty surrounding us. First, knowledge of the line of sky-
and earth-forms, and from this the conception of line and
form of architecture, painting and sculpture. All art, does it
not come originally from the first human consciousness of
the nobility in the lines of the human body?"

"I feel this to be true," you replied, "for when we study a
noble human body we can feel how from this form as first

idea all noble forms may follow as natural sequence."

Then I explained, "Would it not seem to you that when one's idea of the human form is a noble one, so one's conception of all the lines and forms would be ennobled thereby, and that, on the other hand, a weak or false conception of human form would lead to a weak and false conception of all line and form?

"Well then," I continued, "have we not come about in a circle to my reason for saying that to gain a true conception of the highest beauty woman must first gain the knowledge of the true line and form of her own body?"

"But," you asked, "how is woman to learn the correct form of her body?"

"Think of all you have learned in your life," I replied, "and tell me which are the things you have learned best—those which you have read in books or those which you have lived, experienced?"

"Surely," you answer, "those which I have myself experienced.

"Shall a woman find this knowledge in the gymnasium, exercising her muscles, or in the museums regarding the perfection of sculptured form, or do you mean by the continual contemplation of beautiful objects and the reflection of them in her mind?"

"These are all ways," I replied, "but the chief thing is, she must use this beauty and her own body must become the living exponent of it—not by the thought or contemplation of beauty only, but by the living of it—and as form and movement are inseparable as all life is movement, I might say by that movement which is in accordance with the beautiful form will she learn, for in their gradual evolution form and movement are one."

"And how would you name that movement which is in accord with the most beautiful human form?"

"There is a name, the name of one of the oldest of the arts—honored as one of the nine Muses—but it is a name that has fallen in such disrepute in our day that it has come in our country to mean just the opposite of this definition. I would name it The Dance."

"Oh," you cried sympathetically, "so woman is to learn beauty of form and movement through the art of the dance?"

"Yes, and I believe here is a wonderful undiscovered inheritance for coming womanhood, the old dance which is to become the new. She shall be sculptor not in clay or marble but in her body, which she shall endeavor to bring to the highest state of plastic beauty; she shall be painter, but as part of a great picture she shall mingle in many groups of new changing light and color. In the movement of her body she shall find the secret of right proportion of line and curve and —the art of the dance she will hold as a great well-spring of new life for sculpture, painting and architecture."

"Then before woman can reach high things in the art of the dance, dancing must exist as an art for her to practice, which at the present day in our country it certainly does not—that is, according to your definition—for you were speaking of woman's form in its highest beauty, and of a movement which would be appropriate to that form, and you called the practicing of that movement as an art, the dance. But I suppose all art must have some fountainhead from which to draw. And the great fountainhead of movement, where are we to look for it?"

"You ask this," I replied, "as if woman were a thing apart

and separate from all other life, organic and inorganic, but she really is just a link in the chain and her movement must be one with the great movement which runs through the universe and, therefore, the fountainhead, as you express it, for the art of the dance will be the study of the movements of Nature."

A soft breeze came to us from over the sea, the sails slowly filled and took the wind and with the strengthening of the breeze the waters formed in long undulations; for some time our eyes followed them and rejoiced in their movements. Why is it that of all movement which gives us delight and satisfies the soul's sense of movement that of the waves and of the sea seem to me the greatest?

"When the breeze came some moments ago did we both not watch with joy the subsequent movement of the waters and did we not say the greatest movement is the wave movement? The answer would seem to be that this great wave movement runs through all Nature, for when we look over the waters to the long line of hills on the shore they seem also to have the great undulating wave movement of the sea, and all movements in nature seem to me to have as their ground plan the law of wave movement."

The ground, dry baked, heat cracked, the atmosphere of a peculiar hard brightness—overhead the changeless blue sky—through the branches one of the hills—the distance. We are walking together in the pleasant shade of the olive trees, pacing slowly, each filled with our own thoughts. In our walk we reached a gnarled old trunk that had long lain in its present position.

"Do you remember yesterday we were speaking of the movement in Nature and you said that the wave was the great foundation movement of Nature? This idea continually presents itself to me and I see waves rising through all things. Sitting here and looking through the trees they seem also to be a pattern conforming to lines of waves. We might think of them from another standpoint, which is that all energy expresses itself through this wave movement, for does not sound travel in waves, and light also, and when we come to the movements of organic nature it would seem that all free natural movements conform to the law of wave movement. The flight of birds, for instance, or the bounding of animals. It is the alternate attraction and resistance of the law of gravity that creates this wave movement. Do you remember yesterday we were speaking of the dance and when I asked you where you would look for the source of this art, you answered Nature? Since then the idea will not leave me, and I see dance motifs in all things about me. Was this your idea for instance that there is a dance in all Nature?"

"Yes," I replied. "All true dance movements possible to the human body exist primarily in Nature."

"Do you use the phrase 'true dance' in opposition to what you would name the false dance? Is there such a thing as a false dance? And how do you explain this? If the true dance is appropriate to the most beautiful human form, then the false dance is the opposite of this definition: that is, a movement which conforms to a deformed human body. How can this be possible?"

"It sounds impossible," I replied, "but take your pencil and see if we can prove what I have said. First draw me the form of woman as it is in nature. And then draw me the form of woman in the modern corset and satin slippers used by our dancers. And now do you not see the movement that would conform to one figure would be perfectly impossible for the other? To the first, all the rhythmic movements that run through water would be possible. They would find this form their natural medium for movement. To the second figure these movements would be impossible on account of the rhythm being broken in the latter and stopped at the extremities. We cannot for the second figure take movements from nature, but must, on the contrary, go according to set geometric figures based on straight lines, and that is exactly what the school of dance of our day has done. They have invented a movement which conforms admirably to the human figure of the second illustration, but which would be impossible to the figure as drawn in our first sketch. Therefore, it is only those movements which would be natural to the first figure that I would call the true dance."

"But what you call 'deformed' is by many people held to be an evolution in form, and the dance which would be appropriate to woman's natural form would be held by these people as primitive and uncultivated. Whereas the dance which is appropriate to the form much improved by corsets and shoes they would name as the dance appropriate to the culture of the present day. These people would be in no way of your opinion in your definition of what you name the true dance. How would you answer these people?"

"Man's culture is making use of nature's forces in channels harmonious to those forces and never going directly against nature. And all art must be intimately connected with nature at its roots—the painter, the poet, the sculptor, and dramatist, but holding it for us through their work according to their ability to observe in Nature. Nature always has been and must be the great source of all art."

[*The Touchstone*, October 1917]

TO SPEAK THE LANGUAGE OF HUMANITY

It would be wrong to call my art Greek. People have supposed I copied the postures and gestures of Greek statues and Etruscan urns. But it seems to me my art is more universal. If I am Greek, it is the Hellenism of Keats' "Ode to a Grecian Urn." Where Greek art is national in a narrow sense, it is not mine. I aim to speak the language of humanity, not the dialect of a folk. For that reason, all kinds of artistically awakened people, irrespective of nationality, have found a kindred spirit in me. There was Ethelbert Nevin*, for instance. When he heard I was dancing to his music, he came to expostulate with me. "But see her dance first!" pleaded my mother. So I danced for him. It was an ancient Greek story. When I had finished, he rushed up to me and threw his arms round me. "My dear child," he exclaimed, "what you do in the dance is what I dreamed of when I wrote that music!"

It is here [*placing her hand on her breast*] that the center of inspiration lies, and [*placing her hand on her brow*] it is here. All kinds and conditions of people have imitated my work. But they seem to think it consists in certain stereotyped gestures. In reality, it has its virtue in certain soul-states which are, in a sense, incommunicable. The eurythmics of Jaques-Dalcroze** are an illustration of the error that is born of imitation unsupported by original thought. They are good up to a certain point, but they are not creative.

[San Francisco *Examiner*, 26 November 1917]

---

* Ethelbert Nevin (1862-1926). American composer.
** Emile Jaques-Dalcroze (1865-1950). Swiss composer and teacher of "eurythmics," a once popular system of exercise largely derived from Isadora's dance.

THE FREEDOM OF WOMAN

If my art is symbolic of any one thing, it is symbolic of the freedom of woman and her emancipation from the hidebound conventions that are the warp and woof of New England Puritanism.

To expose one's body is art; concealment is vulgar. When I dance, my object is to inspire reverence, not to suggest anything vulgar. I do not appeal to the lower instincts of mankind as your half-clad chorus girls do.

I would rather dance completely nude than strut in half-clothed suggestiveness, as many women do today on the streets of America.

Nudeness is truth, it is beauty, it is art. Therefore it can never be vulgar; it can never be immoral. I would not wear my clothes if it were not for their warmth. My body is the temple of my art. I expose it as a shrine for the worship of beauty.

I wanted to free the Boston audience from the chains that bound them. I saw them before me, shackled with a thousand links of custom and environment. I saw them chained by Puritanism, bound by their Boston Brahminism, enslaved and hidebound in mind and body. They wanted to be free; they cried out for someone to loose their chains.

They say I mismanaged my garments. A mere disarrangement of a garment means nothing. Why should I care what part of my body I reveal? Why is one part more evil than another? Is not all body and soul an instrument through which the artist expresses his inner message of beauty? The body is beautiful; it is real, true, untrammeled.

It should arouse not horror, but reverence. That is a difference between vulgarity and art, for the artist places his whole being, body and soul and mind, on the throne of art.

When I dance, I use my body as a musician uses his instrument, as a painter uses his palette and brush, and as a poet uses the images of his mind. It has never dawned on me to swathe myself in hampering garments or to bind my limbs and drape my throat, for am I not striving to fuse soul and body in one unified image of beauty?

Many dancers on the stage today are vulgar because they conceal and do not reveal. They would be much less suggestive if they were nude. Yet they are allowed to perform, because they satisfy the Puritan instinct for concealed lust.

That is the disease that infects Boston Puritans. They want to satisfy their baseness without admitting it. They are afraid of truth. A nude body repels them. A suggestively clothed body delights them. They are afraid to call their moral infirmity by its right name.

I don't know why this Puritan vulgarity should be confined to Boston, but it seems to be. Other cities are not afflicted with a horror of beauty and a smirking taste for burlesque semi-exposures.

[1922]

SHORT STATEMENTS

This is what we are trying to accomplish: to blend together a poem, a melody and a dance, so that you will not listen to the music, see the dance or hear the poem, but will live in the scene and the thought that all are expressing.
[1898]

℃

When I am rich I shall rebuild the Temple of Paestum and open a college of priestesses—a School of the Dance. I shall teach an army of young girls who will renounce, as I have done, every other sensation, every other career. The dance is a religion and should have its worshippers.
[1901]

℃

My ideal would be to found a temple of ancient art in which, as a sacred priestess, I would devote my life to the worship of the beautiful. I am actively working to promote my idea of the reconstruction of the ancient dances and the ancient dress, and their adoption by as great a number of my sex as possible.
[1903]

℃

The Art of the Dance is a very great thing and what I am doing is only the beginning. It is like a little girl making her first steps. I hope to do better next year; and I hope above all to teach young pupils who will outstep me and realize all that I have foreseen.
[1904]

℃

While my dancing owes inspiration to the Greeks, it is not Greek really, but very modern—my own idea. I shall use Gluck's "Iphigenie" music in New York. I have tried adaptations of old Greek music and found it very unsatisfactory. I once had a choir of Byzantine boys sing old Byzantine music for me, but I found that I couldn't dance to it. I put my trust in modern musicians.

[1908]

Other artists spend more than [my] school will cost on their jewels. Well, this [school] is my jewel.

[1911]

[In my dance] the artifices of dancing are thrown aside, the great Rhythms of Life are enabled to play through the physical instrument, the profundities of consciousness are given a channel to the light of our social day. These profundities of consciousness are in us all.

[1917]

Drawing by staff artist for the Danish journal *Politiken,* 1906

The following statements date from 1920-1927.

All my life I have only "listened to music." I have never been a dancer; I do not like any kind of dancing except, perhaps, the Japanese.

ℭ

No pose, no movement, no gesture is beautiful in itself. Every movement is beautiful only when it is expressed truthfully and sincerely. The phrase "the beauty of line" is—by itself—absurd. A line is beautiful only when it is directed toward a beautiful end.

ℭ

A school for dancing has always been my dream. But in America numberless schools have been founded by people who use my methods without understanding them, and teaching pupils everything they should not do in the dance. I suppose America prefers foreigners to me because I am an American. However, every artist worth anything has always been vilified. It is the price the world demands for the beauty we evoke.

ℭ

A dancer, if she is great, can give to the people something that they will carry with them forever. They can never forget it, and it has changed them, though they may not know it.

ℭ

I went to a musical comedy the other night. Everyone was laughing. But I cried. The waste was terrible to me. It was ghastly to see beautiful young girls come out on the stage saying meaningless words and making meaningless gestures, when they could have been taught to be a force to the nation.

꒰

Thank God the Boston critics don't like me. If they did I should feel I was hopeless. They like my copies. I give you something from the heart. I bring you something real.

꒰

Rodin, the sculptor, was not understood until he was eighty years old. My imitators make caricatures of my dances. They dance with the arms and legs, but not with their souls.

꒰

America is so flippant. They talk of me flippantly. They imitate my dancing, but do not understand it. I preach freedom of the mind through freedom of the body: women, for example—out of the prison of corsets into a free, flowing tunic like this.

꒰

There is nothing new in my Art, which I danced as a child. No one seems to understand, but I am trying to teach the world to think as I do. I have the idea I was born with, and my idea is the idea of life.

꒰

I hate dancing. I am an *expressioniste* of beauty. I use my body as my medium, just as the writer uses his words. Do not call me a dancer.

꒰

Isadora dancing in the Theater of Dionysus, Greece, 1907
(Courtesy, The Bancroft Library, University of California, Berkeley)

I want to start a dancing school in America. By music and the dance I want to train children how to live. I don't want to train them for the stage. I hate children on the stage— though they would be better there than in the gutter.

℧

Place your hands as I do on your heart, listen to your soul, and all of you will know how to dance as well as I or my pupils do. *There* is the true revolution. Let the peoples place their hands in this way on their hearts, and in listening to their souls they will know how to conduct themselves.

℧

Let them give me five hundred, a thousand children, and I will make them do wonderful things! The child is the harmonious instinct, the total freshness; it is the virgin clay wherein can be imprinted joy, life, nature. All children can dance if one knows how to guide them and make them understand what the dance should be.

☽

If I were only a dancer I would not speak. But I am a teacher with a mission.

☽

I believe, as Jean-Jacques Rousseau did, that it is unnecessary to worry a child's brain during the first twelve years of its life. One should offer poetry, music, dancing, not book-learning, during that period. The spiritual experiences last a lifetime.

☽

The children of Communists still receive an essentially old-fashioned bourgeois education. If you want the future generation to understand the nature of Communism and the International, you must today free the child from the slavery of bourgeois education and prejudices.

☽

When building a new world and creating new people, one must fight against the false conception of beauty. Every trifle in everyday life, in dress—every label on a box—must train the taste.

☽

The thing that interests me most in the world is the education of children. All problems can be solved if one begins with the child.

☽

There is no better way to put happiness into the hearts of children of the people than to teach them to dance.

C

When I was twenty, I loved the German philosophers. I read Kant, Schopenhauer, Haeckel and others. I was an intellectual! When I was twenty-one, I offered my school to Germany. The Kaiserin responded that it was immoral! The Kaiser said it was revolutionary! Then I proposed my School to America, but they said there that it stood for the vine, and Dionysus. Dionysus is Life—is the Earth, and America is the land where they drink lemonade. And how can one dance on lemonade? I then proposed my School to Greece, but the Greeks were too busy fighting the Turks. Today I propose my School to France, but France, in the person of the amiable Minister of Fine Arts, gives me a smile. I cannot nourish the children in my School on a smile. They must live on fruits and milk and the honey of Hymettus.

C

When I speak of my School, people do not understand that I do not want paying pupils; I do not sell my soul for silver. I do not want the rich children. They have money and no need for Art. The children I long for are the orphans of the war, who have lost everything, who no longer have their fathers and mothers. As for me, I have little need of money. Look at my costumes. They are not complicated; they did not cost very much. Look at my *decors*, these simple blue curtains I have had since I first started dancing. As for jewels, I have no need for them. A flower is more beautiful in the hands of a woman than all the pearls and diamonds in the world.

C

By dancing thus, and by witnessing such dances, people stay young. Anyone who dances as I do can live to be 100 years old.

Drawing by José Clara

I wanted very much to have five hundred boys and five hundred girls in my School. For my School is a school of life and not a school of dancing. It is a current opinion that dancing is feminine, and therefore only girls have joined my School. But personally, I would have preferred boys, for they are better able to express the heroism of which we have so much need in this age.

℃

Before I die, I want to teach hundreds of children how to let their souls fill their growing bodies with music and love. I never taught my pupils any steps. I never taught myself technique. I told them to appeal to their spirit, as I did to mine. Art is nothing else.

Watercolor drawing by Auguste Rodin

REVOLUTIONARY RUSSIA

Commissar N. I. Podvoisky and Isadora Duncan, Moscow, Summer 1921

"I salute the birth of the future community of International Love."

Long before the October Revolution of 1917, Isadora had proclaimed her wholehearted revolt against the existing order. In *My Life* she asserted that she was "already a dancer and a revolutionist" at the age of five!

Her early radicalism received a powerful impetus when, on a tour of Russia in 1905, her carriage came by chance on funeral marchers carrying the coffins of workers massacred on the infamous "Bloody Sunday." In her autobiography she wrote of this experience: "With boundless indignation I watched these poor grief-stricken workmen carrying their martyred dead . . . If I had never seen it, all my life would have been different. There, before this seemingly endless procession, this tragedy, I vowed myself and my forces to the service of the people and the downtrodden."

It is thus not at all surprising that she welcomed the overthrow of the Czar in February 1917, and the Bolshevik seizure of power eight months later.

In the Spring of 1921 she was invited by the Soviet government to establish her School in Moscow, and she readily assented. "Here at last is a frame mighty enough to work in," she wrote in "Moscow Impressions," a series of letters in *The Art of the Dance*, "and for the first time in my life I feel that I can stretch out my arms and breathe." It filled her with "joy and pride," she added, that she had been called on to aid the "destruction of the old world of class injustice" and the creation of a new world free of exploitation, poverty and war.

During her stay in Russia Isadora "danced the Revolution" more explicitly than ever. She choreographed a dance for the great workers' battle-song, the *Internationale;* two funeral marches in memory of Lenin; and a series of dances inspired by popular revolutionary songs from around the world, including Ireland's

Wearin' o' the Green and France's *Carmagnole.* Her young Russian pupils performed these new dances for large cheering audiences all over Russia, Siberia, China—and after Isadora's death, in France and the U.S.

She hoped to recount the "tremendous experience" of her long Soviet sojourn in a book to have been titled *My Bolshevik Days.* But she had hardly begun that worthy project before it crashed on the shores of everyday life.

"Our First Night in Moscow" and the concluding five titled texts in this section are reprinted from *Isadora Duncan's Russian Days;* the others appeared in various periodicals during her lifetime.

Students of Isadora's Moscow School with workers' children at the Red Stadium, 1924. The banner reads: "The Red Stadium of Trade Unions and the Young Communist League;" the School slogan, "A Free Spirit Can Only Exist in a Freed Body;" "Duncan School."

I WILL GO TO RUSSIA

I will go to Russia to realize, perhaps, the one dream of my life—to have my own theater, with my own orchestra, and an audience that does not have to bargain for seats, and many pupils who will not have to pay for their education. Leonid Krasin* has invited me to establish a national school in Russia. I did not make a contract. I have had enough of contracts. I am going on July 1st.

The Russians have been misrepresented. They may not have enough to eat there, but they are determined that art, education and music must be free to all. I am eager to see if there is one country in the world that does not worship commercialism more than the mental and physical education of its children.

Perhaps I am becoming a Bolshevik. But all my life I have wanted to teach children, to have free schools and a free theater. America rejected this, but there they still have child labor, and only the rich can see the opera, and beauty is commercialized by theater managers and motion picture magnates. All they want is money, money, money.

[Spring 1921]

---

* Leonid Krasin (1870-1926). Russian Bolshevik leader; from 1919 engaged primarily in Soviet diplomatic work.

I SHALL NEVER HEAR OF MONEY:
LETTER TO A.V. LUNACHARSKY*

I shall never hear of money in exchange for my work. I want a studio-workshop, a house for myself and pupils, simple food, simple tunics, and the opportunity to give our best work. I am sick of bourgeois, commercial art. It is sad that I have never been able to give my work to the people for whom it was created. Instead I have been forced to sell my art for five dollars a seat. I am sick of the modern theater which resembles a house of prostitution more than a temple of art, where artists who should occupy the place of high-priests are reduced to the maneuvers of shopkeepers selling their tears and their very souls for so much a night. I want to dance for the masses, for the working people who need my art and have never had the money to come and see me. And I want to dance for them for nothing, knowing that they have not been brought to me by clever publicity, but because they really want to have what I can give them. If you accept me on these terms, I will come and work for the future of the Russian Republic and its children.

Isadora Duncan

[Spring 1921]

[*To this letter Lunacharsky telegraphed in reply, "Come to Moscow. We will give you school and thousand children. You may carry out your idea on a big scale." Isadora telegraphed back, "Accept your invitation. Will be ready to sail from London July 1st."—Ed.*]

---

* Anatoly Lunacharsky (1875-1933). Russian Marxist writer, critic and theorist; a leader of the Bolshevik Party, prominent in October Revolution; Commissar of Education, 1917-1929; sympathetic to the literary/artistic avant-garde; a good friend of Isadora's during her sojourn in USSR.

A GREAT STEP FORWARD:
ARTICLE IN L'HUMANITE

I love the man who creates higher than himself and perishes in this way.
—Nietzsche, *Thus Spake Zarathustra*

You await my impression of Moscow. I cannot, after the manner of H. G. Wells and other writers who have been here, give you political impressions. I know nothing about politics. I can only give you my impressions as an artist, and these impressions are more felt than reasoned.

In each human being, and above all in children and artists, there exists a sixth sense which enables us to divine the psychology of a soul, or a group of men, or a town. It is this sixth sense which has dictated all my artistic career. It was in listening to this voice that I left Europe, where Art has been crushed by commercialism. And it is by this sixth sense that I divine Moscow. For one cannot judge what has happened here in looking about one at the material things. It is with clairvoyant eyes that one must look. For all that is on the surface here is only momentary, and the truth is deeply hidden in the interior of the soul of the country. It is to that great collective soul that the miracle offers itself.

I am convinced that here in Russia is the greatest miracle that has happened to humanity for two thousand years.

We are too close to it to understand, and it is probably only those who will be alive in a hundred years who will understand that by the reign of communism humanity has made a great step forward from which it can never go back.

Moscow is a miracle city, and the martyrdom submitted by Russia will be for the future that which the crucifixion

was. The human soul will be more beautiful, more generous, and greater than ever dreamt by Christ.

I repeat, we are too close to all this to understand.

Had we lived at the time of Christ we would not have
understood, either. We would have seen a simple man
followed by poor disciples, and his crucifixion would have
seemed to us like a banal catastrophe.

And yet the spiritual truth was quite otherwise.

The spiritual truth of that which passes here I see as a
shining vision of the future. The prophesies of Beethoven,
of Nietzsche, of Walt Whitman are being realized. All men
will be brothers, carried away by the great wave of liberation that has just been born here in Russia.

This is the message that my soul received, given to me by
the prophetic voices that arise out of Communist Russia.

This is the message I would like to send to you.

Isadora Duncan

[*L'Humanite*, French Communist Daily,
Spring, 1921]

OUR FIRST NIGHT IN MOSCOW

I went to Russia accompanied only by my pupil Irma and my faithful maid Jeanne who, though livid with fear, would not desert "Madame." We had been told such terrible things that as the train passed the red flag at the frontier, we would not have been surprised if the pictured Bolshevik with red flannel shirt, black beard, and a knife between his teeth, had appeared to violate us all three, and then cut our throats as an evening's amusement.

We all confessed to some shiver of excitement and were perhaps a bit disappointed when there appeared only a very timid young man with gray eyes and spectacles, who said he was a communist student and spoke six languages, and asked if he might serve us. He was very shy and not at all our preconceived idea of a Bolshevik. Only I noticed that when he spoke of Lenin, his gray eyes blazed behind his glasses, and his whole slight figure trembled with enthusiastic devotion. He told, in shivers, of the fanatic sacrifices of the communists and the repulses of the White Armies, which savored of miracle and holy war.

Our first night at Moscow we left Jeanne in the one room available at the hotel, in the one bed, weeping hysterically because she had seen *"des grands rats,"* and we spent the night with a little Bolshevist, wandering about the mystically beautiful city of the many churches and golden domes. He talked, more and more inspired, of the future of communism, until by dawn we were also ready to die for Lenin and the cause.

Then some clouds blew up, and it began to rain on us. Our guide seemed supremely indifferent to the wet, and I

also noticed now that we hadn't eaten anything for four-
teen hours. I found, after meeting others, that a real communist is indifferent to heat or cold or hunger or any
material sufferings. As the early Christian martyrs, they
live so entirely in ideas that they simply don't notice these
things. But Irma and I were worn out, and so we tramped
back to the train.

[mid-1920s]

ИЗАДОРА ДУНКАН.

ISADORA DUNCAN.

Издание Школы Дункан.
20 Пречистенка 20
МОСКВА
1921.

Program of Isadora's performance at the Bolshoi
Theater, Moscow

THE SPIRIT OF RUSSIA:
INTERVIEW IN *SOVIET RUSSIA*

The spirit of Russia is the only sane thing in Europe. All the other countries are thinking in terms of ancient hates and grudges; Russia alone looks to the future. America is the only other country in the world that has its gaze fixed on the future. That is why America should understand Russia.

They [*meaning the government immigration authorities who had tried to prevent her return to her native land*] say I am a propagandist; that I will preach revolution. I am not a politician, I am an artist. But I will try in my dancing to help America to understand the magnificent spirit of Russia. The spirit which after five years of war and famine is without hate or bitterness. The most magnificent thing in the world today.

The spirit of Russia is the spirit of the common people everywhere. So sincere. Groping for Beauty.

I remember before I left America down on the East Side, when my pupils danced, the poor people in the audience cried and begged me to stay and teach their children to dance as my pupils did. But I couldn't; I had no school, no support. For a school such as I dreamed of I needed the support of a government. So I went to France. There, when I talked of my dream of a school where the children would live to dance, I was laughed at.

And so I went to Russia. The Commissariat of Education placed a wonderful house and grounds at my disposal. At first I had nearly a thousand children in my School. But the terrible famine came on and the government could not give me food enough for so many, and all but twenty were sent home. Those twenty were the most talented of all my pupils. I have hopes of bringing them to America. They could show to America, far better than I, what the spirit of Russia is.

Life in Russia is very hard and so art suffers, but out of the universal suffering has grown a common understanding, a spirit. All are equal in suffering; all are drawn closer together through suffering—that is what I mean by the spirit of Russia.

The man who is most conscious of that spirit is Lunacharsky, Commissar of Education. I have seen him in the dead of night tramping through the snow in Moscow, head in the air, totally oblivious to all his surroundings, turning over in his head some plan for the future.

Always, in Russia, it is the future.

[Interview with Karl Pretshold,
Soviet Russia, official organ of the
Friends of Soviet Russia, New York,
15 November 1922]

A COMMISSAR

There is a man* who lives on a hill which rises from a bend of the river. From this hill he overlooks all Moscow and the surrounding plains. He overlooks the shining golden domes, the colored globes, and the crosses of the many churches, and the huge towers of the Kremlin, and in his imagination he peoples the city and the plains with a great new race. There he sees in the vision the glorious youth which will be created for the country of the International. Like Prometheus, this man would give to humanity the flame for its regeneration.

On the hill where he lives stands an immense ruined palace, which was built for one of the favorites of Catherine the Great. Its sturdy walls have withstood the wear of centuries, but within the ceilings have crumbled, and the floors remain but scaffoldings. From its topmost dome waves the red flag of the Revolution, and the man that lives on the hill looks up at this flag, his eyes shining with love, and he says: "By the force of this flag this palace will be rebuilt, transformed into a temple, and it will be inhabited by three thousand youths and maidens, who will here become strong and splendid athletes. A great band to work with free minds and perfect muscles for the future of mankind."

He points down to the Kremlin, and says: "Here will be a mightier stronghold than the old Kremlin has ever been."

---

* Nikolai Ilyich Podvoisky (1880-1948). Russian Bolshevik leader; Party member from 1901; served in Petrograd Military Organization, 1917; Chairman of the Military Revolutionary Committee during the October Revolution; one of Isadora's close friends in the USSR.

And as we hear the church bells of Moscow all chiming together, he says, with an indefinable expression of sweetness: "Other bells will ring for other services."

As his voice ceases, we hear the singing of boyish voices and see tramping down the hillside toward the river a hundred naked youths. These are his first disciples. They live here on the hillside, five hundred strong, in tents. Young soldiers for the new battlefield in the fight for the creation of a finer, more beautiful mankind.

As the man, Comrade Podvoisky, stands there on this high balcony of the great ruined palace, the red flag waving in the free heaven above his head, he looks down on his troops with an infinite love and clairvoyance in his eyes, such as one does not meet in the eyes of a human being, but only dreams of in the eyes of a god; and indeed, seeing him standing there with this strong dream of a new world in his eyes, I turned to my companion and said: "This great revolutionist, this finest of communists, Comrade Podvoisky— this is a godlike man."

[1921]

A MEETING WITH COMRADE PODVOISKY

At Verabyovy Gory I was lying on the grass. I looked up and saw, framed against the sky, a face which made an impression of strength, imagination, and a peculiar sweetness. This was the Comrade Podvoisky, who had seen me from his house nearby and came to greet me. His strong hands raised me to my feet, and I looked into his eyes, brilliantly blue, one moment hard and the next very soft and laughing.

"Now that you have come here you are my prisoner," he said. "I command all the Red Armies, so I can also commandeer you. You are to stay here and give us your Idea. I have heard of your Idea. It has gone all over the world."

"But how can my Idea be of use to soldiers?" I asked.

"What! You do not know that we have here new soldiers?" he said. "The *naked soldier* [athlete] without uniform and without weapons. And women soldiers, too. On the top of the hill there, in the wood, is the camp of youth. There are five hundred youths, and girls too, living in the out-of-doors there in the valley. We are building a great stadium for fifty thousand people. Next summer it will be ready. We are preparing great festivals, dancing, songs, music. On the other hill, where you see that great round castle, we are preparing a house for two thousand children, who will be raised according to the ideals of the new world. You must stay and help us with all this. Look, here come my young soldiers: They are coming down to the river to swim."

I looked. From the heights, descending, came a hundred young boys. They were naked, wearing only little bathing drawers. They were singing: They looked wonderful step-

ping down the wooded slopes to the rhythm of their singing. They were followed by a group of girls. I was sorry to
see the girls wear bloomers and shirt-waists. They didn't
look as fine and free as the boys. I told Podvoisky at once
that the bloomers were all wrong, and the swimming
drawers, too. I told him they ought all to wear short tunics
like Achilles, and the girls should not follow after the boys,
but that they should dance down the hill together, hand in
hand. I asked what the song was they were singing. He
translated. The words were something like this:

> *Death to Speculators!*
> *Death to Parasites!*
> *We are the new free army of the earth!*

" 'Death to Speculators.' You see," said Podvoisky, "that
is why the boys walk first. They have grim work to do, and
perhaps we have not come to the dancing stage yet. These
are the soldiers of the Revolution!"

Podvoisky lives in a simple log cabin with his wife and
five little children, the youngest a baby. They all live with
Spartan simplicity; the children go barefoot all summer.
Once, when inspecting the ruined castle, his little boys ran
right over a floor covered with broken glass. I tried to keep
them back, but Podvoisky stopped me.

"They are future soldiers of the Revolution," he said.
"They must learn to be afraid of nothing."

They say the Bolsheviks are bandits. Podvoisky is a high
Commissar. He might, if he wanted, live in luxury in a
palace, with a Rolls-Royce. All these things are at his disposal, but he prefers to live in two bare rooms, and he eats
every day exactly the same rations that every soldier eats.

He said to me:

"That is why my soldiers follow me and listen to me, because they know that, war or peace, I share the same hardships and eat the same food as they do. And that is why, when the White Army was near, and we were a mere handful of half-starved soldiers, we could force them back. It was because my soldiers knew that, for the Ideal, I had lived and suffered and starved just as they. And so they were ready to follow me to death, or anywhere!"

And as Podvoisky spoke to me, I felt just as one of his soldiers; that I could follow him to death, or anywhere. Podvoisky is a great heroic soul. A man with a heart and pity resembling Christ, with a brain like Nietzsche's and a vision like the men of the future.

Once in his bare room I gave his children a lesson in dancing. He said: "Isadora, it is wonderful. I hardly know my children. In one hour they are transformed. But I am afraid you would soften them, They must be raised, you know, as soldiers of the Revolution."

"Yes," I said, "that is fine, but how can my dancing soften them? I will teach them great heroic movements. Your girls will dance, and your boys will dance like Sophocles before the armies, and inspire them to new deeds of heroism."

"Well," he replied, "if you will teach them such dances, you yourself must live more heroically. Isadora, Europe has somewhat spoiled your fine heroic spirit. Many years of success have softened you. I recognize the spirit, but you must come here and live with us as we live. Then you will be complete."

Alas! I flushed before the spare figure, the Christlike face, the heroic eyes. What was I, a poor pagan sybarite, used to soft beds, good food? Alas! Alas! Why is it that the artist and the saint are so far removed? Never has a saint been an artist and never has an artist been a saint. Fra Angelico, Saint Francis: Yes, the exceptions that prove the rule.

One night Podvoisky took me to the top of the mountain and showed me a ruin. "There," he said, "once stood a fashionable restaurant. The rich bourgeoisie of Moscow, after they had dined sumptuously and exhausted their pleasure with the ballet, used to drive out here and sup with champagne and gypsies until four or five in the morning. Now it is a ruin."

I looked over the black cinders and saw the moon rise over the golden dome of the Church of the Redeemer away in the distance.

"What you say is true," I replied. "Of the sacred gifts of life these people knew nothing. With gypsies and champagne they drowned their consciences. Of the people of Russia, of the children of Russia, they never thought at all."

"Now follow me," said Podvoisky. He took my hand and led me to the beginning of a little path that descended the mountain. As we went down, the path grew more steep and more and more difficult. My feet slipped. I confess I became frightened. The branches tore my dress, my arms, and I feared to fall. It was very dark. Podvoisky gave me his hand: "Lean on me, follow me." Then the stones slipped beneath my feet; the path became more and more difficult, precipitous. I adored the genius of Podvoisky, but I admit I began to feel some anger against him for bringing me down this dangerous and impassable path. After a while we arrived near the river. I was completely exhausted, and I turned to Podvoisky with some reproach, when I heard his voice.

"Dear Isadora," he said, lifting my hand to his lips, "I have taken you down this little tortuous path; it is a symbol. I wanted to show to you how, if you wish to remain in Russia, your way must be down just such a narrow, steep path. In your life you have known great theaters with applauding publics. That is all false. You have known *trains de luxe* and expensive hotels. That is all false. Ovations— false. All false. Now you've come to Russia. By this little dangerous way, I wanted to teach you that if you want to work for Russia, such must be your way. Not the grand opera house, orchestra, applauding publics. No, no, that will lead to nothing. If you want results for your work, go, go alone amongst the people. Dance your dances in little barns in the winter, in open fields in the summer. Teach the people the meaning of your dances. Teach the children. Don't ask for thanks!"

[1921]

Children in Isadora's Moscow School. Drawings by Dana in *Theatrical Moscow*

MAY DAY

The first of May in Moscow was a wonderful sight. The streets were like crimson roses. Thousands of men, women and children, with red handkerchiefs about their heads and red flags in their hands, swept by singing the *Internationale.* All these people had lived for four years on black bread and gray rice but I fancy that that first of May meant more joy to them than every year of good feeling under the reign of the Czar. It was a great sight, those crowds, joyous and confident, singing:

> *The Earth shall rise on new foundations,*
> *We have been naught, we shall be all!*

As I looked and listened I wished with all my heart that this song could be radioed around the whole Earth.

[1922]

NOTES ON SCRIABIN*

The two sources of Art: Apollo and Dionysus.

Music since the time of Bach has been under the influence of Apollo.

Liszt's music is Apollonian. It always seeks for the beauty that comes to human beings from without. Beauty, but a weaker beauty for humanity than Dionysus can inspire.

Scriabin Dionysian.

In his music you will quickly see that his creative strength comes from within.

Liszt's *Les Funerailles,* a human being reaching for happiness and each time falling crushed to earth again.

The Legend of St. Francis d'Assisi. The soul of this beautiful human seeing the brotherhood of man in all nature.

In the *Requiem* of Beethoven and the *Parsifal* of Wagner the human being is resigned and humble before Fate.

With Scriabin begins a new epoch when the human being defies Fate.

Scriabin's *Fourth Sonata.* First Movement. The human being lies in the center of the earth, earthbound.

Second Movement. He dances, expressing earthly joy, but his eyes are drawn out to the universe.

Third Movement. The discovery which comes to the human being of an understanding of the universe giving him the highest ecstasy.

Scriabin is one of the precursors of the revolution and a prophet of it—with music, not words.

---

*   Alexander Scriabin (1872-1915). Russian composer. Lunacharsky wrote in 1925, "We have in Scriabin's music the greatest gift of musical romanticism of the revolution."

Scriabin is a bridge from the old world to the new. He himself took no active part in the building and the conquering of the new world, but he made a great breach in the gigantic wall that stood between the two worlds.

I am also trying to make another breach in the wall, like Scriabin.

I believe that my School will create a new art or show the way toward it. Only the new generation will be able to express the new world and find new genius and new ideas.

It is impossible for me to teach this. You must do it yourselves. Because everything that has been has belonged to the old world. I myself am from the old world and greet the new world that had its birth here.

[1924]

Isadora with students and Irma Duncan at her left;
at her Moscow School, 1921

COME CHILDREN, LET'S DANCE:
SPEECH AT THE KAMERNY THEATER, MOSCOW

When you see these children dancing, I implore you not to view them as little actresses against a backdrop of theatrical scenery. I want you to see them against a backdrop of *nature*, where they can dance freely on the meadow and among the trees.

I am showing you now only a small group of children, because the house where our school is currently situated has only a small dancing hall, with room for not more than twenty children. But that is not enough. I want to give to the future thousands of happy and healthy children.

[At this point the children of Isadora's School danced Schubert's *Requiem March*]

What fine, beautiful children they are, aren't they? But I want all the children in Russia to be like that. After books, after their studies, I want to say to them all: "Come children, let's dance!" I want every child in Russia to have this naturalness, this joy, this beauty which is rightfully theirs. I am sorry that at present I can give my art and my work only to such a small group.

Have you ever read Jean-Jacques Rousseau's *Emile*? He says there that a child lives each day an intense and beautiful life, and that we must give the child the possibility of making use of it. I don't "teach" children. I have no special systems and methods. I don't say to the child, "Hold your hand like this, or put your foot like this." You have seen for yourselves that every child dances naturally. You saw that their movements are not taught—they grow like plants, they unfold like flowers.

Little children don't understand verbal teaching. Words, for children, are not alive. Children learn through movements; up to the age of ten or twelve they learn more from the soul. But nobody believes in the soul any more, so I say they learn from the spirit, or from intuition. I have observed that even the smallest children understand Beethoven and Schubert. But they could never understand them through words—only through movements. Movements form themselves as naturally as plants, with all their feelings. A child's life changes all the time, changes continually. Every pedagogue who really wants to do so adapts himself to the child, who is like a plant: never static, always growing. The pedagogue should give the child something new every day.

Today you have seen how every child expresses the same dance in a different way. Each child must be approached separately, because every child is different.

I hate muscles, arms and legs. I never tell a child to "hold yourself so; do this." I do not like physical culture and sports. I do not like the Dalcroze system. I regard all that as sin—a crime against the nature of children. A child needs something very different. It needs naturalness, without pressure, and without influence. There is no need to subject a child to any demands. The child should, by itself, unfold like a plant to the light, to the sun.

Here in our head is knowledge, thought; here in our breast is a motor supplying power for our most wonderful emotions. I say to the child, "Put your hands here on your breast, then lift them high and higher to the stars, to the planets. Embrace the whole world with your arms. Reach out to the universe! You are only a small child, but you stand on the Earth. There is a place for you in the universe."

Some Communists have told me that all this is "mystical"—that arms outstretched to the stars are "mystical." But I teach the children to look up above them, to look around, to be conscious of the whole universe: Is that mysticism? No, I have no mysticism. I say to the child, "Look at the world—the whole universe dances together with you, the human being. Man, different from all the other animals holds up his head, while his feet remain on the Earth."

Soon the children will come before you with simple movements, and you must imagine that it is night and that they are looking at the stars. I say to the children, "When you run out into the woods or into the garden, try to keep yourselves free, in harmony with nature. Go and enjoy yourselves—jump, play, laugh and be boisterous." But I am not of the opinion of some of your pedagogues, that children ought to be left entirely to themselves, screaming and fighting each other like wild Indians. No, the child must learn self-control—to express its feeling harmoniously. That will make it grow stronger than those children who are left to grow up wildly without learning to control themselves. To let a child develop itself through a dynamic dance is difficult, but to make it hold its musical pause—as the children have just done in the Schubert march they danced for you—is still more difficult. I have noticed afterward that they gained more strength from that than from the dynamic dance.

I want very much to know your opinion of my educational system. [*Loud applause*]   The greatest compliment to my School would be if every mother in the audience said, "I too would like my child to dance like that."

I came to Russia to create something big, something grandiose. The word *Bolshevik*—meaning *big*, I thought—inflamed me when I heard it in Europe. I imagined that it would be possible to create a school of a thousand children here. All I needed for that was a big place in which to work. And now three years have passed, and I have waited in vain.

When I came to Russia, I did not intend to give public performances. During these three years I have asked those in power to give me a large heated place in winter, and a large arena in summer, where I could teach my art to a thousand children. These children here, that you have just admired, are mostly children of workers and peasants. Are they not beautiful? And does it not prove that they can be cultured and intelligent?

I desire to give the greatest joy and the greatest beauty to the children of the workers—to make them so perfect that they will be envied by the children of the millionaires. You have surely heard the legend of Cornelia, where pearls and diamonds are compared to the natural beauty of children. I would like to have the workers say, when they see thousands of children dancing in a great folk festival: "These are our jewels!"

I am afraid I have tortured you this evening with my lecture. You would have preferred, of course, to see the children dance some more. But as it was our intention to show what we have achieved so far, your slight suffering was necessary, and might even prove to be the foundation for the future School.

[Excerpts; 1924]

DANCING IN THE RED STADIUM

This summer the children of my School who have lived and studied here for three years under the most difficult circumstances, enduring cheerfully a life of hardships, held a meeting and decided that in spite of the fact that they have no material wealth of any sort, they were rich. So rich that they felt the need to give to others of their treasure.

They decided that they would call a meeting of a hundred children of workers, and teach them the art which had given themselves a new Life and Beauty. The meeting took place on the great sports ground of the Red Stadium, at whose head is the Comrade Podvoisky. With the help of the Comrade Podvoisky these classes were organized, and every afternoon of the last three months of this summer our brave little class of forty have taught hundreds of children to dance.

Children who come to the first meeting pale and weak, who could at first hardly walk or skip or raise their arms to the sky, have become transformed under the influence of the air, the sunshine, the music, and the joy of dancing, taught to them by the young pioneers.

Their costume is a simple red tunic, without sleeves, and ending above the knees. I watched these hundreds of children dancing; sometimes they resembled a field of red poppies swaying in the wind. At other times, seeing them rushing forward together, one perceived that they were a band of young warriors and amazons ready to do battle for the Ideals of the New World. But the best of all was the enthusiasm and the happiness of the children themselves. How they loved to throw themselves heart and soul into these beautiful movements; and when song was added to the dancing, it seemed that their entire being was lifted in exaltation of the complete and joyous rhythm of youth.

Movement is a language even as powerful and expressive as words. I could not explain my lessons in words to these children, but I spoke to them by the language of movement and they by their responsive movement showed me that they understood.

"Children, place your hands here, as I do, on your breasts; feel the life within you. This movement means *Man*." The children answered in chorus: *"Chelovek."* "And now raise the arms slowly upward and outward to the heavens. This movement means *Universe*." The children chorused: *"Vyselenaia."* "Now let your hands fall slowly downward to the earth." And the chorus responded: *"Semlia."* "Now hold you hands toward me in love and this means *Comrade*." Chorus: *"Tovarish."*

[1924]

SHORT STATEMENTS

The Soviet is the one government that cares about art nowadays—and about children.

☽

I expect to spend ten years in Russia. I will give my art to the Russians, whom I adore, and who will support me with splendid musicians and disinterested enthusiasm.

☽

I left Europe where art is closely linked with commerce. And it will be contrary to all my convictions and wishes if I shall again have to give paid performances to a bourgeois public.

☽

I have given my hand to Russia, and I tell you to do the same. I tell you to love Russia, for Russia has everything that America lacks, just as America has everything that Russia lacks. The day when Russia and America understand each other will mark the dawn of a new epoch for humanity.

☽

I love the Russian people and intend to go back there next year. Nevertheless, it is very comforting to return to a place where one can have warm water, napkins, heat, etc. One has other things in Russia but, poor weak humans that we are, we become so accustomed to luxuries that it is very difficult indeed to give them up. Not that the Russians believe in giving up luxuries! On the contrary—but they believe in *luxuries for all,* and if there is not enough to go around then everyone should have a little less.

☽

If more could be known of these great men [the Bolsheviks] who gave every ounce of their vitality, brains and souls for the great cause, Russia would be far more respected today. A Communist must live on the highest plane.

C

My three years of Russia, with all its suffering, were worth all the rest of my life put together. There I reached the highest realization of my being. Nothing is impossible in that great weird country.

[1921-1927]

A. V. Lunacharsky spoke at this performance by Isadora and the pupils of her School; Theater of Musical Drama, Moscow

LIFE WITH ESENIN

Isadora and Serge Esenin, New York, Spring 1922

"The only world that is worth living in—the Imagination."

In his *Anthology of Sublime Love,* surrealist poet Benjamin Péret called Serge Esenin "the greatest Russian poet of modern times." It is an estimate that has been frequently seconded.

Of peasant origin and upbringing, Esenin (1895-1925) was a central figure in a Russian avant-garde group, the Imaginists, so-called because of their insistence on the primacy of the image in poetry. His finest works, *The Hooligan's Confession* and others, resound with a boisterous, desperate lyricism. When Isadora met him in 1921, he was already one of the best known poets in the USSR.

Their turbulent life together has been misrepresented year after year in volume after volume. Fortunately, in Gordon McVay's *Isadora and Esenin*—an effort to understand the "tangled relationship" of the two artists, "and the role they played in one another's lives" (see Bibliography)—we have a sympathetic and impeccably researched account that supersedes all that has been written on the subject.

With the exception of her "Last Will," all the pieces in this section were published during Isadora's lifetime. The statement "Greetings to the American People" appeared, with slight variations, in several U.S. newspapers. The extent of Isadora's authorship of it cannot be determined, but it is probable that she wrote at least some of it; it was she, in any case, who read it to the assembled reporters when their ship landed at New York harbor on the first of October, 1922.

It should be noted that long before Esenin's suicide he and Isadora had been separated; they may not even have seen each other for two years.

Isadora and Esenin Berlin 1922

LAST WILL

This is my last will and testament. In case of my death I leave my entire properties and effects to my husband, Serge Esenin. In case of our *simultaneous* death then such properties to go to my brother, Augustin Duncan.

Written with clear conscience.

Isadora Esenin-Duncan

Witnessed by   I. I. Schneider
                    Irma Duncan

May ninth, 1922, Moscow

GREETINGS TO THE AMERICAN PEOPLE

Here we are on American territory. Gratitude—that is our first thought. We are the representatives of young Russia. We are not mixing in political questions. It is only the field of art that we are working. We believe the soul of Russia and the soul of America are about to understand each other.

We are come to America with only one idea—to tell of the Russian conscience and to work for the rapprochement of the two great countries. No politics, no propaganda!

After eight years of war and revolution, a Chinese wall is surrounding Russia. Europe, itself torn by war, hasn't enough strength to tear down that Chinese wall. Russia is in the shadows, but it is misfortune that has helped us. It is during the Russian famine that America made a generous gesture. Hoover has destroyed the Chinese wall. The work of the American Relief Administration is unforgettable.

Above everything else I wish to emphasize the fact that today there are only two countries in the world—Russia and America.

In Russia there is an avid thirst to study America and her sweet people. May it not be that art will be the medium for a new Russian-American friendship? May the American woman with her keen intelligence help us in our task!

On the journey here we have crossed all Europe. In Berlin, Rome, Paris and London we found nothing but museums, death and disenchantment. America—our last but greatest hope!

Greetings and thanks to the American people!

[1922]

I APPEAL:
LETTER TO THE *NEW YORK HERALD*

Dear Sirs,

I appeal to the Law and ask you to correct certain errors in your front page article appearing in the *New York Herald* yesterday, February 16th.

You state that my husband, Serge Alexandrovich Esenin, returned to our apartment at the Hotel Crillon and after breaking up everything in the apartment proceeded to throw articles of toilet at me. *This is not true,* as the night porter of the Crillon can attest. I left the hotel immediately on the entrance of Esenin, in company with my friend, Madame Howard Perch, with the object of calling to the aid of Esenin, Doctor Jules Marcus. The crisis of madness which Esenin was suffering is not altogether due to alcohol, but is partly the result of shell-shock during the war; terrible privations during the Revolution brought to the present crisis; and also blood poisoning caused by the drinking of Prohibition whiskey in America—of this I have the attestation of a celebrated doctor of New York, who treated Esenin during different similar crises in that city, and who told me in case of recurrence to send at once for a physician.

Esenin is one of the many victims of America's Prohibition laws, from which one can read daily cases of death, blindness or insanity.

When Madame Perch and I returned to the Crillon with Doctor Marcus, Esenin had already been taken from the hotel. I write this in justice to Esenin, whom you have twice falsely stated as having attacked me. I know it is the politics of American journalism to make a joke of the matter of grief and disaster, but truly the young poet, who from his eighteenth year has known only the horror of war, revolution and famine, is more deserving of Tears than Laughter. I think all Mothers will agree with me. Serge Esenin is a great poet and in his normal state a most beautiful spirit, whom all his friends adore. Of him Gorky said to me: "Since Gogol and Pushkin, we have not had so great a poet as Esenin." Alas! Gogol died insane, Pushkin was killed at an early age; the Fate of Poets is marked with tragedy.

On our former stay in Paris, Esenin and I dined with Madame Cecile Sorel and many other friends, where the drinking of good French wines only inspired Esenin with happy thoughts. He admired and loved Paris—and continually exclaimed, "How lovely! This is real culture. Here all is Beauty!"

As you can imagine, what has happened has left me profoundly grieved and desolate. I brought Esenin from Russia, where the conditions of his life were of terrible hardship, to save his genius for the World. He is returning to Russia to save his reason, and I know that there will be many hearts all over the world who will pray with me that this great imaginative poet may be saved for future creation of that Beauty which the World so needs.

Sincerely,

Isadora Duncan

P.S.—By the way, since the name of George Washington is America's Holy Symbol for truth, why do you falsely state that there was no whiskey to be had in that boat?

Esenin received as much bad whiskey in that boat as he did in every other place in America, in every town in which we traveled, constantly offered to him by hundreds of sellers of poison.

Vive la Verité! Vive la sagesse Française! Et les bons vins de la France!

[*New York Herald,* Paris Edition, February 1923]

[*The* George Washington *was the ship on which Isadora and Esenin returned to Europe.—Ed.*]

Serge Esenin, 1922

THE TRUTH OF THE CASE:
LETTER TO THE *CHICAGO TRIBUNE*

Dear Sir,

In the course of the last week there have appeared in the *Chicago Tribune* three front-page articles in which my name has been used in large disrespectful headlines and in which my character has been put in an extremely false light before the public. As the incident which is the supposed subject of these articles was of so slight a nature as in no way to be of interest to the public, I conclude that these articles were inserted on your front page simply with the object of injuring me, and I insist upon my right, according to the laws of France, to your publishing my reply in the same column and the same page as the articles in question.

In your article of February 16 you declare that there was between my husband, Serge Alexandrovich Esenin, and myself "another domestic row," whereas if you had taken the trouble to learn the truth you would have known that the explanation of the incident of the Hotel de Crillon was that Esenin was seized by a fit of deliriums, that there had been no quarrel of any sort between us, as my friend, Mrs Howard Perch, who was with us all afternoon and evening can testify, and that at the moment of Esenin's fit of madness, I was not in the hotel, having presaged what was coming.

I had left with my friend, Mrs Perch, to call a doctor.

All this was explained to your reporter, Mr Lorimer Hammond, by Dr. Aszoule, chevalier of the Legion of Honor, but Mr Hammond preferring to write, and only looking for a scandalous and defamatory article, paid no attention to this information.

The exact truth that Serge Esenin is the unfortunate victim of momentary fits of madness, at which moments he is no longer responsible for his actions or his words, was too simple a solution for your reporter who was looking for scandal.

Two days after, this same Mr Hammond penetrated my retreat at Versailles, where I lay in bed ill under the care of the doctor. The doctor forbade me to see him. Mrs Perch told him this, to which he replied that the article coming would be "worse if I did not see him."

Hearing this, and wishing so far as I could to protect the character of Serge Esenin from further harmful writings, I rose and, putting on a dressing gown, went into the next room. I saw at once from the attitude of Mr Hammond that he had come with hostile intentions to continue his attacks on me and my unfortunate husband.

I explained to him as gently as I could the truth of the case and that I was very tired and in great sorrow. Of all this the next day he was pleased to make a huge joke in a most unpleasant article. If this sort of journalism continues, we will have your reporters coming into no matter what house of misfortune or grief and making a joke at tears of the mourners. They will be opening the coffin lids and describing in humorous fashion the expressions of the dead. No one will be safe from their malice, and the poor public will be the continued dupes of their gross and uncomprehending vulgarity.

Hoping that your paper will in the future refrain from this unworthy policy, I remain,

Isadora Duncan

[*Chicago Tribune*, Paris Edition,
28 February 1923]

LIES:
LETTER TO THE JOURNAL *L'ECLAIR*

Sir,

Mr Serge Esenin and I wish to protest against the lying writing published by Monsieur Merejkowski* in *L'Eclair* of the 16th of June.

Monsieur Merejkowski says:

1st Lie

"Mr Serge Esenin and Madame Isadora Duncan were expelled from America and then from France." This is a lie. Not only were we *not* expelled from America, but my representations in Carnegie Hall were attended seven times by audiences of 4000 enthusiastic persons, who acclaimed me with bravos for a half hour after the program—enthusiasm little known in America. What then does our deportation consist of?

2nd Lie

Our "deportation from France"—the while we are living very happy in our house.

Monsieur Merejkowski then writes, on the subject of my Art, that my tired legs amused the public at the Trocadero.

To this I can only reply that I have never sought to amuse the public, my one desire being to make them feel what I myself am feeling. And sometimes I have succeeded. But my legs are the least of my means for, being neither an acrobat nor a dancer, I have the pretentions of being an *artiste*. And even were I legless I might still create my Art.

---

* Dmitri Merejkowski (1865-1941). Russian author; lived in Paris after 1917; wrote *The Causes of Decadence in Modern Russian Literature, Jesus the Unknown,* and, with his wife Zinaida Hippius, *The Reign of the Antichrist,* a portrayal of Bolshevik Russia.

3rd Lie

Monsieur Merejkowski dares to say that I am beaten by my "young husband." It is a happy thing for Monsieur Merejkowski that he is protected by his great age, otherwise Esenin would force him to eat those words. Esenin says: "*Yest starry, starry*—he is old, old. Were he not I would make him answer for his insults."

4th Lie

Monsieur Merejkowski says that during a spectacle at the Trocadero I called Lenin an angel. The truth is I called Esenin an angel, for he is the man I love. I did not speak of Lenin, and if I had spoken of him I would have said, "He is a man of genius," but I never would have called him an angel.

Moreover, I have nothing to do with politics.

During the war I danced the *Marseillaise,* because I felt that it was the road that led to Liberty.

Today I dance to the sound of the *Internationale* because I have the feeling that it is the Hymn of the Future and of Humanity.

I went to Moscow, allured by the great art dream of directing a school with a thousand children; after a year's work I feel I sowed some joy and some good about me, and with the memory of that I spoke of a Poet and the little children who are hungry.

In the *Nouvelle Revue* of the 15th of May, 1923, Mr Brian Chaninov has written: "At the present time and since the death of Alexander Blok, who died in 1921, Esenin is incontestably the most celebrated, if not the greatest poet in Russia. This young man is a natural force." This is the poet that Monsieur Merejkowski would like to stigmatize by calling him a "drunken *moujik.*"

Edgar Allan Poe, the glory of American poetry, was a dipsomaniac. And what can be said of Paul Verlaine,

Baudelaire, Moussorgsky, Dostoyevsky, and Gogol, who died in a madhouse? Yet they all left works of immortal genius.

I quite understand that M. Merejkowski could never live in the proximity of such beings, talent always being shocked by genius. In any case, I wish for M. Merejkowski a very peaceful old age in his bourgeois retreat, and a respectable funeral with black plumes and black-mittened hired mourners.

As for me, I prefer being burned alive at the stake in Moscow, while thousands of children in red tunics dance about me singing the *Internationale.*

"Russia will be reborn," writes Merejkowski. Does he not know that Russia has just been reborn, the first miracle since Jesus Christ?

And it has not only been the Renaissance of Russia, but that of all the Earth, of Humanity, of the Future.

Isadora Duncan

[1923]

ON ESENIN'S SUICIDE:
TELEGRAM TO THE PRESS

The news of the tragic death of Esenin has caused me the deepest pain. He had youth, beauty, genius. Not content with all these gifts, his audacious spirit sought the unattainable, and he wished to lay low the Philistines.

He has destroyed his young and splendid body, but his soul will live eternally in the soul of the Russian people and in the souls of those who love the poets. I protest strongly against the frivolous and inexact statements printed in the American press of Paris. There was never between Esenin and myself any quarrel or divorce. I weep his death with anguish and despair.

[January 1926]

SHORT STATEMENTS

While I slept my soul left my body and ascended into the world where souls meet—and there I met the soul of Serge. We fell in love immediately, as souls, and when we met in the flesh we again loved and were married. Not only was ours a love marriage but it was also a marriage which united Russia and the United States.

℃

Serge is not a politician. He is a genius. He is a great poet.

℃

[In Russia] he is called the greatest poet since Pushkin.

℃

Serge is the Walt Whitman of Russia.

℃

Every child is born a genius, I think. Those whom the world calls geniuses, when they grow up, are to my mind simply the children who have happily escaped education. Here is a genius [*turning to Esenin*]. Here is young Russia. Mad as a hatter, strong, full of vitality. Poetic!

℃

I never believed in marriage and now I believe in it less than ever. I married Serge only to enable him to get a passport to America. He is a genius, and marriage between artists is impossible.

Serge loves the ground I walk on. When he goes mad he could kill me—he loves me so much more, then. For four months I worked with Serge. He is the loveliest boy in the

Drawing of Isadora and Esenin by Victor Barthe

world, but a victim of fate. Like all geniuses, he's cracked. I've given up hope of ever curing him of his occasional madness.

All his friends [know that Serge has been] subject to extreme nervous attacks. All poets are like that, but that doesn't prevent him from being a wonderful genius and a beautiful character.

Yesterday I saw an attack coming on and went to get a doctor. When I returned the room was wrecked. It was then I thought it would be better for him to return to Russia.

Some Russians can't be transplanted, you know. That was the tragedy of Nijinsky. Serge is like that.

℃

The press will one day regret the way it has treated me, and if I commit suicide it will be as a protest against the brutality of the press. My husband was a Russian, and all Russians break furniture when they are drunk. Is there a single great writer, apart from Goethe, who did not have vices? My husband and I were not divorced, as the papers write, for I was only married according to Soviet law, the best and most natural law in the world. I am a poor, misunderstood woman, and my heart is pure. Now the whole world smiles, but I weep.

The first five statements made in 1922; the next two in 1923; the last in December 1925.

LOVE
AND
LIFE

Reading Ernst Haeckel's *Anthropology*. Photograph by Gordon Craig

"I am a Yogi of the Epicurean School."

Isadora was what is called a voracious reader, especially of poetry, drama, mythology, philosophy and the history of the arts. Although her formal education was limited, her interest in ideas and her quest for knowledge were boundless. In *The Real Isadora* Victor Seroff remarked: "Having in my possession a part of her library, I can attest to the thoroughness of her studies on the evidence of the volumes annotated in her own hand."

Her highmindedness and intellectual sincerity contrast with the vulgarity of so many of her commentators, particularly on the subject of love—a subject central to her life, and on which she had important things to say.

In an article published in *The Mentor* for February 1930, George Seldes—later to become one of the last but best known American "muckrakers"—reported that "in a low moment" in 1924 Isadora had the idea of publishing the love letters sent to her by many famous men over the years. She planned to publish a selection of these letters in a book to have been titled *What Love Means to Different Men;* her aim was not only to raise sorely needed funds for her School, but also "to show mankind it does not know how to love." Of this project there remains only a draft of the preface, "Love and Ideals." Perhaps there is no better antidote for the poisonous gossip that has flowed so liberally from the pens of so many of her biographers and critics than this little-known statement, dictated in a mood of dark despair.

The enigmatic lines published here as "A Poem" appeared originally in Arnold Genthe's album of photographs, *Isadora Duncan: Twenty-Four Studies* (see Bibliography). The "Statement to the Press" was her published response to the many thousands of letters she received on the death of her children.

Photograph by Arnold Genthe

A POEM

Nietzsche signed his
   last telegram
"Dionysos crucified!"
Perhaps am I La Madonne
qui monte le Calvaire
   en Dansant.
O Dionysos, Porte-Flambeau,
Light me the way in flames—
    I S A D O R A

[undated]

STATEMENT TO THE PRESS

My friends have helped me to realize what alone could comfort me—that all men are my brothers, all women my sisters, and all little children on this Earth my children.

[New York Times,
29 April 1913]

Drawings by Aspell, 1898
(Courtesy, Russell Hartley, The Archives for the Performing Arts)

PRESENTIMENTS

Two months before the death of my children the presentiments began. Every night on entering my studio I saw three large blackbirds flying around. I was so much troubled by the apparitions that I consulted a doctor, who said that my nerves were upset, and prescribed a tonic.

But while I was touring in Russia the idea continued to haunt me and became so strong that I thought my own death was imminent.

One night before going on the stage I wrote my will and enclosed it in an envelope marked "To be opened in the event of my death."

Later, while making a long railway journey, I heard Chopin's "Funeral March" throughout the night, and had a vision which was so vivid that I danced it the next night just as I saw it, without previous rehearsal.

I was told that everybody in the theater wept. I replied: "Yes, it is strange."

My impression was that I was walking to my own tomb. I felt the icy wind and afterwards I experienced an ecstasy which did not seem to be of this world.

Now I ask whether the word "accident" means anything. Disaster walked toward me. I felt it. Three times it was foretold. Was this only hazard?

[New York Times,
10 August 1913]

APPEAL FOR FUNDS
FOR THE RELIEF OF THE CHILDREN
OF FRENCH ARTISTS

It is impossible for those who have not been there recently to realize the poverty there is in Paris. I wish to get money for those who are not relieved in the ordinary way by charities, and who cannnot plead for themselves.

Not only the children of stage people but families of musicians are in need. These artists have never saved money. To them the sun was always shining, and they gave liberally to their poorer brethren.

[Excerpts; November 1914]

Drawing by Jean-Paul Lafitte

LOVE AND IDEALS

I find it difficult to write this book. I find it hard to speak when I know that every word is being taken down. I want this book to be something worth leaving behind. It will be worth doing only if it is a book which will help people to live. I want to tell the truth about my loves and my art because the whole world is absolutely brought up on lies. We are fed on nothing but lies. We begin with lies and half our lives at least we live with lies. Most human beings today waste some twenty-five to thirty years of their lives before they break through the actual and conventional lies which surround them.

I am not an artist at all. Artists bore me to death. All the singers you meet talking about the A-flats they can reach— all the violinists and pianists talking about the size of their audiences and the writers about the size of their royalties. They give me no pleasure at all; these artists are stupid. At a concert the only artist present is the man who wrote the music they produce; at a play, the author of the text. Theater artists are silly and egotistical persons. All artists as a rule are much overrated.

Art is not necessary at all. All that is necessary to make this world a better place to live in is to love—to love as Christ loved, as Buddha loved.

That was the most marvelous thing about Lenin: *he* really loved mankind. Others loved themselves, money, theories, power; Lenin loved his fellow men. They say to me, "How can you be so enthusiastic about Lenin? He did not believe in God." I reply: "That is simply a phrase. Lenin was God, as Christ was God, because God is Love and Christ and Lenin were all Love."

Do *you* love mankind? Lenin did. That's why he was supreme—because he really loved. When the world once really understands this it will be a tremendous thing, because most people really love nothing.

And that is why I want to publish this book—not for money, but because I want to show mankind it does not know how to love.

What mankind calls love is only hatred in another form. In the flesh there is no love. I have had as much as anyone of that sort of thing which men dare call love—men foaming at the mouth—men crying they would kill themselves if I didn't return their love: love—rot! I had just barely come to the stage when it all began—this declaration of love. From all sides I was besieged by all sorts of men. What did they want? Their feelings, I know now, were the same feelings they have for a bottle of whiskey. They say to the bottle, "I'm thirsty. I want you. I want to drink you up. I want to possess all of you." To me they said the same things: "I am hungry. I want you. I want to possess you body and soul." Oh, they added the soul, all right, when they pleaded for the body!

Was that love? No. It was hysteria.

Love is the rarest thing in the world. Even a mother's love is largely egotistical. A cat loves her kittens up to a certain age. People talk of a mother's love as the most sacred thing in the world—why, it is just like loving your own arms and legs. It is simply loving a part of yourself. That is not the love I wanted. I wanted a pure, unselfish love, the love for humanity felt by Christ and Buddha and Lenin.

When I was in Moscow I saw little children lying huddled asleep in doorways and on rubbish heaps. Would this be possible if there was love in the world? I took these children into my school and let them sleep there. After Lenin died the Soviet Government would no longer allow this. Was that love?

Did you ever go to the East Side of London? What did you see there? If you did not see children actually sleeping in the streets as in Russia, you must have seen them under conditions terrible enough. If there is such a thing as love in the world, would people allow this sort of thing? Could they go to their comfortable homes knowing that there are children living in such distress? So long as little children are allowed to suffer, there is no love in this world.

Men have loved me but my only love has been children. All scientific men, all doctors, are amazed at what I have accomplished with children. First of all, I take them very seriously. All children are very serious beings, despite the fact that their parents and their teachers treat them as ignorant and inconsequential little animals. They come to me with all sorts of troubles mental and physical. Many have rickets and bone disease. When I started my first school in Berlin, Geheimrot Professor Doctor Stoffer came to look at my pupils, and when he saw them he exclaimed: "These children are not for you. They are for me—they are in need of surgical care. This is not a school; it is a hospital. You will never make these children dance."

And you should have seen the children dance after a year! Simply because I let them do what they liked. I let them dance—I did not ask them to dance. Then I inspired them to better dancing, that is all. They grew and thrived and blossomed.

Of course, it may be egotistical after all. Oh, there is nothing like it. You feel a sort of god, you know. Prometheus! It is marvelous to be able to form human lives! I have taken these children from the lowest proletariat, weak and diseased and destined for misery and early death—the children of men who dig ditches and break stones on the highways—and before I left Moscow they were dancing in the Grand Opera and the people had arisen and cheered while they cried.

Once you are interested in shaping children's lives you will never be interested in anything else again. There is nothing greater. I have never taken a grown-up pupil or a paying one. I worked only when I could work for nothing.

The world calls me a dancer. It says I have revived the classic art of dancing of the Greek era. But I am not a dancer. I never *danced* a step in my life. I hate all dancing. All I see in what people call dancing is merely a useless agitation of the arms and legs. I don't like to look at stage dancing. But I can understand ballroom dancing—the tango, for instance, as danced in Buenos Aires. It is quite wonderful there, in the little cafes with the low ceilings; it has a meaning. The man dances with the same girl all the evening, and if another man tries to dance with her he runs a dagger through the stranger's back. This is the sort of dancing based on sexual desire and the right of possession. We see all the outward movement. But what of the inward movement, the movement of the mind? I am not a dancer. What I am interested in doing is finding and expressing a new form of life.

I see only the ideal. But no ideals have ever been fully successful on this earth. Ideals always bring calamities in their wake. People with ideals frequently are driven mad.

You follow an ideal, devote your life to it, and you may go mad—yet what else is there? Nothing except ideals. Everything else is like having a good meal: It passes the time in a very charming manner and satisfies one of the principal desires of the flesh. That is all.

Every two thousand years there come certain phases in human conditions and certain forces renew themselves. Ideals incarnate. We have Dionysus and Christ and Buddha—and the force of the present epoch is Lenin. I am certain that in a thousand years from now people from all parts of the world will come to Lenin's tomb, which will be a shrine. He was the person who embodies the new spirit, the renewal of the force of idealism and the new religion.

I went to Russia because I am interested more in the time hundreds of years from now than the present. A practical person going to Moscow sees only calamity and general catastrophe. This condition followed the crucifixion of Christ and must follow Lenin. In ages from now people will realize this. Now they see only what is taking place—I saw the Ideal.

[*The Mentor*, February, 1930]

SHORT STATEMENTS

Certain persons in your city [New York] have raised $100,000 in order to bring a speaker [evangelist Billy Sunday] to this city to tell us strange things. I am the daughter of Aeschylus, Sophocles, Euripides, Tyndall, Huxley, Herbert Spencer and Walt Whitman—and this speaker tells me that they are all in Hell. Well, I wish he would go to that Hell so that he may speak with authority.

℃

I have been trying for twelve years to get someone to support my School here. I have devoted all that I have made to this cause. I have no capital. I don't believe that people should have capital. Their worth should be in themselves.

℃

This [Metropolitan Opera House, New York] is not a democratic theater. I would like to see a theater where there were no first tier boxes, second tier boxes and galleries . . . . The people on the East Side would enjoy the nine symphonies of Beethoven if they did not have to sit on the ceiling to hear them.

℃

The one man in America who seems to have understood my art as I understand it is a Russian Jew who writes for a paper on the East Side of New York.

℃

[Nietzsche's] end was madness. But how do we know that what seems to us insanity was not a vision of transcendental truth? Would Poe have written "Ulalume" if he had not been inspired by alcohol?

One wonderful moonlit night [in Berlin, c.1903] the people took the horses out of my carriage and dragged it to my hotel. When we reached a little park all fringed with marble Hohenzollerns, I ordered them to stop. "Look at those statuesque abominations!" I shouted. "Why will you permit one man, a man with no art in his soul, to force you to contemplate such hideousness?" Then the police interfered.

The statements above are from 1917.

The following statements were made between 1922 and 1927.

There are many who think, apparently, that life is a series of extremely boring habits which they call virtues. I do not believe in putting chains and a padlock on life. Life is an experience, an adventure. It is an expression. Most Americans are hypnotized by a wrong idea of life, brought to this country by the Puritans.

One cannot make plans for life, or rules for marriage. Life comes, and one lives, each day. I am opposed to marriages. I believe in the emancipation of women.

(Courtesy, Russell Hartley, The Archives for the Performing Arts)

That gruesome thing we used to call "middle-age" should disappear. Women, if they will, can prove the power of mind over matter.

ↄ

All my lovers have been geniuses; it's the one thing upon which I insist.

ↄ

I hate charity. Rich men work women blind in sweat-shops, and then endow eye-hospitals!

☽

Art is greater than governments.

☽

The great symbol of America is Walt Whitman.

☽

When in doubt, always go to the best hotel.

☽

Publish my memoirs now? What do you think I am? An old woman? Am I dead? Only the living dead publish their memoirs. Oh, I'll have time enough when I'm dead to write them.

☽

How can we write the truth about ourselves? Do we even know it?

☽

People invent gods to please themselves. There are no others. There is nothing beyond what we know, what we invent or imagine. All the Hell is right here on earth. And all Paradise.

☽

My motto: *sans limites.*

☽

So long as there is the rich child and the poor child, there can be no democracy.

☽

Advice spoken to Constantin Stanislavski*: Mon cher, you are faced with this dilemma: Either you must consider your life at an end and commit suicide, or else you must begin life all over again by becoming a communist.

℃

Yes, I am a revolutionist. All true artists are revolutionists.

℃

Only the solidarity of the working people as exemplified by the International can safeguard the future of civilization.

℃

There is a new idea of living now. It is not home life, it isn't family life, it isn't patriotism, but the International.

℃

Communism is the only solution for the world.

---

*   Constantin Stanislavski (1863-1938). Russian actor, producer and drama theorist; co-founder and director of the Moscow Art Theater.

GOODBYE, AMERICA!

Painting by Alexander Anderson, who used 200 bronze keys to symbolize the fact that Isadora unlocked so many doors to personal freedoms for us all through her Art and beliefs

*"Let's go onwards and upwards,
against all practical reasons!"*

Isadora's last American tour, from early October 1922 to the following mid-January, was a complete disaster. After her ship docked she was ordered to Ellis Island because of her pro-Bolshevik views, and subjected to a stupid, grueling interrogation. Heywood Broun commented: "Anybody but an immigration official would have known that Isadora Duncan is before and after everything else a dancer . . . She is an artist of the first rank, who has revolutionized dancing not only in America but all over the world. She deserves a warm welcome from her own country instead of blundering boorishness."

Blundering boorishness, however, is what she received. In front-page news stories all over the country she was vilified as an "agent of Moscow," with dark hints that she had been "sent" here by Lenin and Trotsky on some secret conspiratorial mission. Church groups, self-styled "patriotic" organizations and countless cowardly writers of anonymous letters-to-the-editor joined in the venomous hue and cry. The mayors of Boston and Indianapolis insulted her; evangelist Billy Sunday called her "that Bolshevik hussy." In many cities her performances were canceled. She was deprived of her U.S. citizenship. And as if all this were not enough, she had constant arguments with the manager of her tour. Esenin, who accompanied her on her voyage, added still more difficulties. Virtually unknown in an unfamiliar country whose language he did not know, the poet was continually depressed during his U.S. sojourn; he was frequently ill, drank heavily, and got into brawls. Finally Isadora was forced to return abroad without having earned any money for the support of her School.

A passionate outcry against the vicious unfairness with which she was treated during those three and a half months, the following texts are also something more: They are a vigorous protest against America's provincialism, puritanism and philistinism—a devastating critique of all that is wrong and rotten in the "land of the dollar."

True to her word, Isadora never again returned to the country of her birth.

In New York, Esenin and Isadora pointing to the Statue of Liberty

AMERICA MAKES ME SICK!

Yes, I am leaving America. I am shaking the dust of your narrow-minded, hypocritical, loathsome United States from my feet.

America makes me sick—positively nauseates me. This is not a mere figure of speech. America produces in me a definite malady—I know the symptoms; I have felt them here on other visits.

Stupid, penurious, ignorant America disgusts me and I am going back to Russia, the most enlightened nation of the world today.

You feed your children here canned peas and canned art, and wonder why they are not beautiful. You will not let them grow up in freedom. You persecute your real artists. You put them under the heels of fat policemen, like the ones who sat on the platform of my concert in Indianapolis. You drug your souls with matrimony. You import what art you have, which isn't much. And when anyone tells you the truth you say, "they are crazy!"

I am absolutely, unutterably and vehemently opposed to all legalized marriage. I think the wedding ceremony is a most pernicious foe to the poor little victims of marriage—the children. If it were not for this dreary, monotonous, miserable, wretched, inane life-mating of humdrum Mrs Brown with crabbed, cranky, shifty Mr Brown, the poor little Browns might have had some chance in life.

What do parents do in their holy wedded life? They

browbeat, intellectually and spiritually, every child that is born to them. They commit malpractice upon the souls of each of their offspring. How can children be expected to grow up in honor, happiness or even common decency when they have to stand the mealtime quarrelings of their parents till they are old enough to leave the parental roof-tree? Oh, I know, some parents think they are enjoying their bickerings and still sparing their children by talking in veiled language. But any child worth the name sees through that talk. Marriage is a failure. Ask Geraldine Farrar*.

Maybe some people may think I do not practice what I preach, since just a year ago I got married myself. Well, I was forced into matrimony by the silly laws of the lands I had to travel through as an artist. I married my husband to get him past the customs officers. I married my husband because if I were not married to him in our—huh! huh!— "free America," two burly policemen would have the right to raid my hotel and take us into court because we were natural enough, and sane enough, and loving enough to live together without this throttling wedding ceremony. That's why I married, and that's only why.

Oh yes, I knew anybody who heard me talk of marriage as the institution which more than all has cursed our country would inevitably ask: "How about the children? How will they be taken care of if the parents don't set up housekeeping?"

I reply: by the State. Every mother should be at liberty to do some sort of decent work for the world, while women

---

* Geraldine Farrar (1882-1967). American dramatic soprano; member of the Metropolitan Opera in New York; her divorce in 1923 was much publicized.

whose life vocation is really children should be educated
into the beautiful profession of caring for children—other
women's, as well as their own. Thus the mothers of the
world would be free to experiment as to fathers for fit
children, as a botanist experiments as to fertilizer for fit
seed. What a preposterous thing that a woman should give
children to the world by only one father! The Russian
Communists have the right idea.

Look at the race of run-down, lily-livered, stoop-
shouldered, dreary-minded American men who yearly are
becoming the fathers of the new generation of little Americans. Why should a woman who is really a mother at heart
have to bear the children of one of these sublimated essen-
ces of fiddle-dee-dees of fathers to the sixth or eighth
child? Why shouldn't she have the right to choose a better
father for her sixth child than she chose for number one?

Perhaps, in some cases the father, in his youth, was fit to
be a father. But in his knock-kneed fifties he is too hard-
headed for anything spiritual to spring from him. Then let
his wife rotate the children crop just as sensible farmers
rotate the crop of potatoes. Let her look about for a young
father, fit to be perpetuated in a child. After all, I should
think the baby crop is quite as important as the potato crop!
But in these somnolent United States, you will never get
our President, our lawmakers, our ministers or our doctors
even, to see the vast wisdom of what I am now setting
forth. You'll all keep on having humdrum children in the
same humdrum bondage of old matrimony.

But it is not alone on the score of the family that I so
object to my native country. I object also because my country has no imagination. When I tell my friends that I love
my husband because, when I slept, my soul traveled off

into space and joyed in finding his soul there, they think I am crazy. When I explain that I was a dancing girl on the Nile ten thousand years ago, and that my husband was then a soldier, and that we two were lovers and merely renewing the ancient associations now again centuries later in the year 1921, they again think I am crazy. Ah, they understand not true love which means to them nothing but a stereotyped wedding-ring.

It's the smugness, the sanctimonious righteousness, the "God bless me and my wife, my son John and his wife, us four and no more, Amen" quality to America which crushes my soul. As for me, I would rather be free than be out of debt. I would rather see with clear eyes than be a millionaire. I remember some years ago a millionaire whom I associated with for eight years. He wanted to marry me. But I shuddered at the stall-fed project.

He took me to France. He bought a chateau. He filled the garage with fifteen costly motors. "Now, Isadora," said the millionaire to me, "marry me, and these are yours."

And I replied: "Is not my love enough, that you should want marriage, too? After we are married, what then?"

"Why," said he, gasping, "why, marriage ends all. We'll just sit down and be happy."

And I spurned the millionaire. "That's the trouble," said I. "I could never be happy, sitting down. I could never be happy with matrimony which always ends it all. I want revolution which cleanses. I want debts, if I must have them; I want suffering and hardships and love that is more cruel than pain. I want life and adventure and the whole world. Who are you, with your millions, to try to capture my soul?"

And I did not marry him. At one time, if I had exacted money in return for my affections, I could have owned

Madison Square Garden. The millionaire would have given it to me. Now what do I get instead? I have had the receipts of my last two concerts attached for debts that were incurred when my life was bound up with that millionaire's. The debts were incurred in my name, of course, but they were his debts. He could pay for them, easily. But the man who offered me stultifying marriage turns a deaf ear now.

The curse of the United States is its humdrum old life, same yesterday, today and always. The curse of my country is its slavishness, mental and spiritual. Most of us in the United States are dead—all dead—at the top. Nothing new and progressive, like the Russian Revolution, can come out of America—just yet, at any rate. We think the same old thoughts about life and love and art that our round-shouldered old grandsires thought, as they twirled their straggled whiskers of an evening, as they sat huddled before the airtight stove. Airtight—yes, that's what we are now, in America. No breeze of progress can ever pierce our airtightness.

Bah! I am tired of the American hypocrites who lift their eyebrows at the barefoot dance; at the exposure of our bodies which should be the temple of god in man. Bah! Bah again! I have had about as much of a chance this winter in America as Christ had before Pilate. We both were doomed before we even spoke. When I think of some of the experiences I have lived through on my American tour it makes me want to be a Christian. It makes me feel even that mean.

Take Boston. In Boston Mayor Curley enunciated some dreary old bromides about indecent bodily exposure and barefoot dancing on the occasion of my appearances in his town. And I came back—and I do come back now, saying I know what is the matter with Boston. Boston—you intelligent, who are still living in America, if there are any of you still living—is in rigor mortis because of its fearful conception of life and culture. I do not know, on the whole, but that I should call it "culchoor" when I speak of it in connection with Boston.

Now in that city, I heard, they objected to me because they thought I was a Red; because they heard I sympathized with the Bolsheviks. I will explain. There are, in the world, persons of three colors. There are the whites. Their color typifies a purity which is useless; a starved quality of the body and mind and emotions from which no young may spring; a sterility which is praised only by its own barrenness. That's your ultra-pure, all over our country.

The next color is gray. They paint the walls of their Symphony Hall gray in Boston because that is the color of polite funerals and hearses where too much sadness is not desired. Gray is the color of Boston—people who are dead and buried already, and past the wreath-hanging episode which comes shortly after the demise. That's Boston. Dead, politely, positively dead, so far as any thought or any feeling, or any quickened intelligence are concerned.

The last color of all is red. That's the color of the people who do the real work of the world. That's the color of the people who have enough *guimpe* to their upper story to ask: "Why? Why? Why?" That's the color of the artists and the creators, the great soldiers and fighters and poets. And that's my color, praise the Lord! For you see, the color of my blood—I am glad, glad to say—is still red, even after my American tour.

I have been in sad financial straits in America. That is one grudge I feel toward my country. She lets her artists starve. And my manager had me by the throat. To save money on the last two concerts, he refused to give me an orchestra. I had to get along with a pianist. It seemed to me that art suffered too greatly if I could not have an orchestra. So I went to a woman who says she is my friend. She is one of the richest women in New York. She has told me, again and again, that my dancing has healed her children's souls. So I laid my need before her.

"How much will an orchestra for the last two concerts cost?" she asked me.

"Twelve hundred dollars," I told her.

She said the income tax was so expensive that she couldn't do this little thing for art. I then sent her a rare piece of lace, the last nice thing I have. I thought if she would buy it I would give my all to make those concerts right. And she sent the lace back by the chauffeur, without even a note. That was all she cared for her children's souls—I had healed them, she said, but they weren't worth two hundred dollars apiece to her, those souls. In these United States we value the unseen things of the spirit in very few dollars and cents.

Of course, later, I got an orchestra of Russian players, thanks to my strenuousness. But that I had to stand a moment's worry on this score is outrageous.

Routine, weary routine, the same old table in the middle of the same old floor, the same old books on the same old table—that's America.

But I will predict. I have seen the Russian revolutionists in Moscow standing in the street, some so poor that their feet are done up in newspapers for lack of shoes. I have seen the freedom in their faces, as they sang the *Internationale,* waving the red flag. I have seen your workers parade, also, down Fifth Avenue. I have watched the poor starved bodies, their weak backs and shrunken limbs. Yet I see, in those downtrodden exploited ones, the promise of America.

Wake up, in time! Or else those crushed will start thinking, from overburdened necessity. And on Fifth avenue, they will start up the *Internationale,* while the red flag is waving all about. After all, since red is the color of youth and promise and vigor and initiative and all virile creation, that may be the only cure possible for these dreary, routinized United States.

[*Hearst's American Weekly,* January 1923]

Drawing by Robert Henri

SHORT STATEMENTS

Before I set foot on Ellis Island I had absolutely no idea that the human mind could worry itself into figuring out all the questions that were rapidly fired at me today. I have never had anything to do with politics. All my time in Russia has been spent taking care of little orphans and teaching them my art.

☽

I feel as if I were acquitted of murder. They [officials at Ellis Island] seemed to think that a year's residence in Moscow had made me a bloodthirsty criminal ready to throw bombs at the slightest provocation. They asked me silly questions such as: "Are you a classical dancer?" I told them I don't know; my dancing is quite personal. They wanted to know what I looked like when I danced! How do I know? I never saw myself dance.

☽

They may keep my body from entering America, but they cannot keep out my spirit. There are at least 20,000 young girls all over the country, from New York to California, who are now dancing the classic dances that I brought into fashion twenty years ago.

☽

There is just one thing that astonishes me. That is to hear that the American government has no sympathy with revolutions. I had always been taught that our great country was started by a revolution, in which my great-grandfather, General William Duncan, played a noble part.

☽

You were once wild here—don't let them tame you!

☊

My manager [Sol Hurok] tells me that if I make more speeches the tour is dead. Very well, the tour is dead! I will go back to Moscow where there is vodka, music, poetry and dancing. [*Pause*] Oh yes, and *freedom!*

"*Isadora Dansant et Jouant de la Flute*,"
drawing by Antoine Bourdelle

I am here [at the Waldorf-Astoria, New York] to rest and recover from the persecution I have suffered from the American press throughout my trip. Every time I come to America, they howl around me like a pack of wolves. They treat me as though I were a criminal. They say I am a Bolshevik propagandist. It is not true. I am dancing the same dances that I did before Bolshevism was invented.

☽

America was founded by a bunch of bandits, adventurers, puritans and pioneers. Now the bandits have the upper hand.

☽

The Ku Klux Klan tried to deport us, but the American Legion is the worst of all. It is the worst bunch of old women I ever met.

☽

I am a Russian now. I was born an American. And if I am a "Red," as they say, then those who go about so busily taking the alcohol out of wine, the beauty out of the theater, and the joy out of living, are *grays*.

☽

I never saw Lenin or Trotsky in all the time I have been conducting a school for Russian children in Moscow. My husband is just a young Russian poet. He is no politician, but a genius.

Our passports are visaed properly and we are not coming here to preach propaganda. We simply want to tell Americans of the children over there, and how they are being neglected.

I tell you, that is all we come for. I wish to let people know how these children live on black bread, and how last

Christmas I saw them dance around a pathetic tree in a room five degrees below zero. I am not concerned with politics or government, but with the Russian children. They are wonderful.

℃

Why is it that my dances are copied in girls' schools all over the country, yet when I appear in person I am subjected to calumny on all sides? They are willing to copy my ideas but not to help the originator.

℃

Why wasn't there something in the papers this morning about my farewell appearance last night in the Lexington Opera House? I suppose they wouldn't give me credit for the reception I received. The audience got up and sang the *Internationale* after the performance.

℃

Every morning here [in the U.S.] when I got up or went to bed, people wanted to know what I ate, what I drank and where I slept. Why, I got up the other morning to find in the newpapers a story that my beloved Serge had given me a black eye in a Bronx flat. It's a darn lie.

℃

The people of this country are physically sick. They believe they are supreme in everything.

℃

Americans would do anything for money. They would sell their souls, their mothers or their fathers. America is no longer my country. Ireland is the country for me, but now Paris is not so bad.

℃

WILL L. GREENBAUM ATTRACTIONS PRESENT

ISADORA DUNCAN

Classical and Symphonic Dancer

"CREATOR OF A NEW ART"

—— ASSISTED BY ——

Symphony Orchestra

of 60

OSCAR SPIRESCU, Conductor

COLUMBIA THEATER

Sunday Afternoon   -   Nov. 25
Tuesday Afternoon   -   Nov. 27
Friday Afternoon   -   Nov. 30

PROGRAMS WILL INCLUDE

Beethoven
Chopin
Iphigenie en Aulide ⎫
Iphigenie en Tauride ⎬ Gluck
Orpheus ⎭
Tschaikowsky

PRICES: Box Seats $3.00;   Orchestra $2.50;   Balcony $2.50, $2.00; $1.50; Gallery $1.00

Americans do not appreciate art. What nation can that permits natural scenery to be destroyed from one end of the country to the other by hideous billboards?

I have been constantly misrepresented during my stay here. First it was the fault of the immigration officials. By holding me at Ellis Island they made it appear that I was a dangerous radical. The papers seized upon this estimate of me and allowed it to color all my future actions. Reporters sent to interview me, instead of asking about dancing, wanted to know what I thought about free love or common ownership of property. I give the Hearst papers especially the credit for making my trip a complete failure.

C

You newspapermen wrecked my career. I'm going back to Russia. I'd rather live on black bread and vodka there than have the best you've got in the United States.

We've got freedom in Russia. You people don't know what it is. Your capitalist newpapers have ruined what promised to be a properous tour for me. I got only as far as Chicago and had to borrow money for my fare back here to New York and to Russia.

C

Freedom here? Pah! Your capitalist press ruined my tour because I came here to teach the people what freedom really is. Your people don't want art. When I arrived here to give you real art they put me on Ellis Island. If anyone here speaks his mind, the government prosecutes him. But they can't stop him from drinking!

As to Prohibition, as they call it, no Prohibition country for mine. Some of the liquor I drank here would have killed an elephant. It would have killed *me*, if I had stayed on much longer. It is possibly a good thing that I am going back to Moscow.

C

I really ought not to say a word to you newspapermen. You have succeeded in ruining my tour, on which I had hoped so much to earn enough money to send back to my starving children in Moscow. Instead of taking back money, I have been compelled to borrow money from friends.

Your papers have devoted whole columns to printing details about my personal life during my tour: what I ate, what I drank, whom I associated with—but never a word about my art. Materialism is the curse of America.

This is the last time you will ever see me in America.

꒰

I am against Prohibition, newspaper photographers and the world in general that lies this side of Paris and Moscow.

If I came here to borrow money, as a foreign representative or banker, I'd get a great reception. But as a recognized artist I get Ellis Island. They treated me as a dangerous revolutionist. Well, I *am* a revolutionist. So is my husband, and so are all real artists.

꒰

I lost four months of my life on my American visit. It was martyrdom.

꒰

Now I am going back to Moscow. That "horrible" Soviet government at least appreciates art. It has endowed a children's school and I will resume my teaching there.

꒰

So good-bye America! I shall never see you again!

A NOTE ON SOURCES

The principal aim of this book has been to collect as many as possible of Isadora Duncan's writings and speeches that are not included in *My Life* or *The Art of the Dance*.

Much of this material is taken from the following magazines: *Current Literature, Hearst's American Weekly, The Mentor, Modern Dance, Soviet Russia* and *The Touchstone.*

Most of the shorter statements are from daily newspapers, including the New York *Globe, Herald, Journal and Advertiser, Sun, Times, Tribune* and *World;* the Chicago *Daily News, Evening Post, Tribune* and *Voice of Labor;* the San Francisco *Examiner;* the Milwaukee *Journal;* the Toledo *Blade;* the London *Daily Herald;* the Paris *L'Humanite;* and the Moscow *Izvestia.*

A few pieces are from unidentified newspaper clippings; a very few are brief quotations cited by Isadora's acquaintances in published memoirs.

This collection contains a number of open letters and letters-to-the-editor; *personal* correspondence, however, has not been included.

"I Was Born in San Francisco," "Continually Surrounded by Flames," "A Meeting with Comrade Podvoisky," the "Speech at the Kamerny Theater" and several shorter texts are reprinted from *Isadora Duncan's Russian Days* by Irma Duncan and Allan Ross Macdougall (New York, Covici-Friede, 1929).

Some of this material has been translated from the French, German, Russian, and Danish.

F.R.

SELECTED BIBLIOGRAPHY

This list includes only English-language books, pamphlets and special issues of journals. Titles marked with an asterisk (*) include letters written by Isadora.

BOOKS BY ISADORA DUNCAN

My Life. New York: Liveright, 1927. Reissued in many editions by other publishers.

The Art of the Dance. Edited with an introduction by Sheldon Cheney. New York: Theatre Arts, 1928, and 1977. Includes essays on Isadora by Margherita Duncan, Raymond Duncan, Max Eastman, Robert Edmond Jones, Eva LeGallienne, Shaemas O'Sheel and Mary Fanton Roberts.

BIOGRAPHIES AND STUDIES

Ballet Review 6, No. 4 (1977-1978). New York. Articles by Jill Silverman, André Levinson, Elizabeth Kendall, Debra Goldman, Julia Levien, Annabelle Gamson and Don Daniels.

Desti, Mary. *The Untold Story: The Life of Isadora Duncan, 1921-1927.* New York: Liveright, 1929.

Duncan, Irma. *Duncan Dancer: An Autobiography.* Middleton: Wesleyan University Press, 1966. (*)

———. *The Technique of Isadora Duncan.* New York: Kamin, 1937; and New York: Dance Horizons, 1970.

——— and Macdougall, Allan Ross. *Isadora Duncan's Russian Days, and Her Last Days in France.* New York: Covici-Friede, 1929. (*)

Dumesnil, Maurice. *An Amazing Journey: Isadora Duncan in South America.* New York: Ives Washburn, 1932.

Genthe, Arnold. *Isadora Duncan: Twenty-Four Studies.* Foreword by Max Eastman. New York: Mitchell Kennerley, 1929. An album of photographs.

Hartley, Russell, and Solomon, Judith. *Isadora Duncan.* San Francisco: Archives for the Performing Arts, 1977. Brochure for a Centennial Exhibition.

Macdonald, Nesta. "Isadora Reexamined: Lesser-Known Aspects of the Great Dancer's Life." Six-part series in *Dance Magazine* (July through December 1977). New York.

Macdougall, Allan Ross. *Isadora: A Revolutionary in Art and Love.* New York: Thomas Nelson, 1960. (*)

Magriel, Paul, ed. *Isadora Duncan.* New York: Holt, 1947; also in *Nijinsky, Pavlova, Duncan: Three Lives in Dance.* New York: DaCapo, 1977. Texts by Gordon Craig, Allan Ross Macdougall, John Martin and Carl Van Vechten.

McVay, Gordon. *Isadora and Esenin.* Ann Arbor: Ardis, 1980.

Rather, Lois. *Lovely Isadora.* Oakland: The Rather Press, 1976.

Roslavleva, Natalia. "The Isadora Duncan School in Moscow," *Dance Perspectives* 64 (Winter 1975). New York.

Savinio, Alberto. *Isadora Duncan.* New York: Rizzoli, 1979.

Schneider, Ilya Ilyich. *Isadora Duncan: The Russian Years.* New York: Harcourt, 1968.

Seroff, Victor. *The Real Isadora.* New York: Dial Press, 1971. (*)

Steegmuller, Francis, ed. *Your Isadora: The Love Story of Isadora Duncan and Gordon Craig Told Through Letters and Diaries.* New York: Random House, 1974. (*)

Stokes, Sewell. *Isadora Duncan: An Intimate Portrait.* New York: Brentano's, 1928.

Terry, Walter. "The Legacy of Isadora Duncan and Ruth St. Denis," *Dance Perspectives* 5 (Winter 1960). New York.

_____. *Isadora Duncan: Her Life, Her Art, Her Legacy.* New York: Dodd, Mead, 1968.

Walkowitz, Abraham. *Isadora Duncan in Her Dances.* Girard, Haldeman-Julius, 1950. An album of drawings and watercolors, with texts by Maria-Theresa, Carl Van Vechten, Mary Fanton Roberts, Shaemas O'Sheel and Arnold Genthe.

INDEX